ZERO DEBT

The Ultimate Guide to Financial Freedom

Lynnette Khalfani

ADVANTAGE WORLD PRESS

Published by Advantage World Press
P.O. Box 452
South Orange, NJ 07079
www.AdvantageWorldPress.com

Printed in the United States of America
First Edition: October 2004
Editor: Tawana Bivins-Rosenbaum

Third Printing: November 2004

Publisher's Cataloging in Publication Data

Khalfani, Lynnette.
Zero debt : the ultimate guide to financial freedom / Lynnette Khalfani. -- 1st ed. -- South Orange, NJ : Advantage World Press, 2004.
p. ; cm.
Includes index.
ISBN: 1-932450-75-0
1. Consumer credit. 2. Finance, Personal. I. Title.
HG3756.U6 K43 2004
332.024--dc22 0410

Other Books by Lynnette Khalfani

Investing Success: How to Conquer 30 Costly Mistakes &
Multiply Your Wealth!

The Zero Debt Workbook (January 2005)

Investing Success for Women (March 2005)

Additional Titles by Advantage World Press

Ready, Set, Grow! 10 Success Strategies
for Winning in the Workplace

by Veronica J. Holcomb

You Can Afford to Retire

by Michael Kresh

SPECIAL SALES

Advantage World Press books are available at special bulk purchase discounts to use for sales promotions, premiums, or educational purposes. Special editions, including personalized covers, excerpts of existing books, and corporate imprints, can be created in large quantities for special needs. For more info, write to:

Advantage World Press, Special Markets
P.O. Box 452
South Orange NJ 07079
Fax: 973-324-1951
E-mail: specialmarkets@advantageworldpress.com.

Acknowledgments

Zero Debt really took shape after a 30-day national tour to promote my previous book, *Investing Success*. At every city I visited, people asked me for ways to get rid of their debts. So I dedicate this book to all those out there burdened with excessive debt, and to those striving to achieve true financial freedom.

To Akil, thank you for your steady stream of advice, for always demanding excellence from me, and for being the type of father our children can forever admire.

To Jakada, my wonderful son: Thanks for your unwavering affection and bright smile. You always make my days better. Mommy also appreciates your keen intellect. How many other 4-year-olds know the four things that can be done with money? I can hear you now saying: "Save, spend, invest or donate it!"

To Aziza, my precious daughter: Everyone who meets you realizes that you are wise beyond your seven years. What did I do to deserve you – my firstborn child – as an eternal blessing in my life? Thanks for keeping me on my toes. So many things I do – or choose *not* to do – I do with you in mind. You make me want to be a better person, become a better mommy, and set a higher standard of what a woman should be. Aziza, thanks also for suggesting a series of money books for kids. I promise I'll write them soon!

To Deborah Darrell, the world's best media coach and strategist. You often tell me that you're proud of me. But I want you to know, sis, that you I look up to you in so many ways. Your discipline, consistency and courage are awe-inspiring. You are setting such a marvelous example for Dylan. Keep making choices (even tough ones) and living your life in a way that you'd want Dylan to emulate, and you'll continue to hold your head high.

To Earl Cox, of Earl Cox & Associates: I couldn't have made it this far without you. Your help, expertise and counsel at every stage of my publishing career have been invaluable. So many authors have benefited from your consulting, agenting, publishing, and book promotion wisdom. You should be proud of the success that you've had in taking your clients to the next level. FYI, I'm thrilled to work with you and look forward to many more productive years together.

And to Tawana Bivins-Rosenbaum: Once again, thanks for your careful eye. I lucked out in having you as my editor.

Table of Contents

Introduction

DEBT. It's the single worst four-letter word in the English language.

Debt is the longest-lasting economic curse, the most heinous financial plague, and the least recognized form of modern slavery afflicting Americans this millennium. Debt keeps you up late at night. Debt drives you to drink, fight with your spouse, have anxiety and experience a host of other miseries that you never imagined. Can't figure out why you're always depressed on the morning after payday? It's because the only ones celebrating your payday are your creditors, since 40% of your paycheck is going towards your ever-growing debts.

Not Getting Ahead?

Despite that paycheck you're receiving, you don't feel like you're really getting ahead, right? You probably feel more like you're drowning in debt. And even for those of you who don't owe a dime on any credit cards, my guess is that you still feel financially insecure. Whatever category you fall into, read on, because *Zero Debt* can help you move from financial anxiety to financial freedom.

When you come home and see that pile of bills in your mailbox, many of you wonder: "What have I gotten myself into?" Admit it: How many times have you received an American Express bill in an over-stuffed number 10 envelope? Felt like you were in the middle of a B-horror flick, didn't it? But the movie wasn't called "I Know What You Did Last Summer." It was more like "I Know What You Blew Your Hard-Earned Money On Last Month."

Are You Robbing Yourself?

Carrying around a load of debt is like robbing yourself bi-weekly without a ski mask. Next payday, I want you to buy a ski mask and wear it when you sit down to pay your bills. That's right, then look at yourself in the mirror ... Ski mask on and say, "easy-come, easy-go money." You finish writing the checks, and then you're flat broke – *again.* To squash your depression, you go fix your poor, miserable self a drink – but it's the cheap stuff because you certainly can't afford the top shelf brand. That thought makes you even more depressed, so you call up one of your girlfriends, and decide to go out for drinks. At the bar/restaurant, you pay $15 per glass for cosmopolitans (yes, $15 a glass; you live in New York City, where everything is ridiculously priced). When the tab comes, you both fight to whip out your credit cards. You win. Then you keep your fingers crossed hoping your MasterCard gets approved. The waiter takes forever to handle your payment. When you finally see him return, he seems to be walking in s-l-o-w motion. By now, you've started to silently pray to God that the waiter graciously says "Thank you, Miss," as opposed to looking at you suspiciously or stating with a stern face: "Ma'am, your card was declined. Do you have *cash* or another card we can use?"

Let's give this tale of horror a semi-happy ending...Yes, the card *is* approved, saving you from public humiliation. But since you

NEVER pay your MasterCard in full at the end of the month (despite your best intentions and contrary to what you and 70% of Americans claim when asked about it), your two rounds apiece of cosmos that ran you $73.95 ... (Keep up with me now: $15 x 4 drinks is $60, plus tax and a 15% tip...You DO tip, don't you?) ... that $73.95 will now be paid over, say, 12 months, at 21.9% interest compounded daily. Translation: those four drinks will really cost you more like $90. And that's just one night out on the town.

If your debts are mounting right now, you know exactly what I mean. But wait, don't kick the cat, or go crying to Mom ... Oh, and put away that ski mask too. Don't even think about it. How does seven to 10 sound? Trust me. It ain't worth it.

The Zero Debt Philosophy

In case you haven't gotten my point by now, let me break it down to you this way: Excessive Debt is bad. Zero Debt is good. I repeat: Excessive Debt is extremely bad. Zero Debt is outrageously good. Sure there are "good" forms of debt – like financing for your house. We'll talk about that later. For now, however, think of Zero Debt as your new mantra, a goal, a higher plane that you aspire to reach ... a state of nirvana where you have complete financial comfort and absolute peace of mind.

You see, with Zero Debt, even someone with a blue-collar salary can obtain white-collar dreams: The white picket fence, the two-car garage, the happy family barbecues, and game nights with everyone watching the 50-inch plasma TV that hangs on your wall.

Yes, even that 50-inch TV you've been daydreaming about can be yours – *if* you play your cards right.

Join the Zero Debt Revolution

This is where I come in. Think of me as your money coach. I want to share with you the secrets of the Zero Debt philosophy. It's not about what you *can't* have, or making you endure unreasonable sacrifice and pain. It's about making smart money moves, and getting a game plan so that you can achieve financial freedom for life.

The Zero Debt revolution is about changing your thinking and learning some unconventional personal finance wisdom. Scores of financial "experts" tell you to cut up your credit cards – as if *not* having credit cards alone will solve your problems. It won't. That's why so many people who *do* cut up their credit cards later wind up in the same predicament, sometimes burdened with even more debt. They haven't had that critical "breakthrough" in their brains – that Aha! moment that makes leads them to permanently change negative money habits. So I don't suggest that you take scissors to your plastic. Frankly, I disagree with that approach. It won't teach you true fiscal discipline or proper credit management. I also won't preach about buying off-brand items exclusively, or only shopping at flea markets – although those last two tactics are useful now and again.

Deprivation Doesn't Work

Do you know anyone who constantly diets but his or her weight still yo-yos all over the place? Some of those people may publicly say "no" to dessert, but then privately, they're pigging out on all kinds of goodies. The reason is simple: They can't stand depriving themselves, at least not for a long time. I realize you don't want to feel deprived either – as if you're on a money diet. At the same time, I know you don't want to be in bondage anymore. And make no mistake about it: if you've got excessive debt, you're definitely in bondage. You're a slave to debt and it's got a terrible grip on you. Well, get ready to knock out that debt for good, so it won't balloon again. Now is the time to take action and permanently slash your debt, because if you're not careful – *really* careful – you or someone you care about is going to get crushed by that debt.

I Don't Have Debt – So This Book Isn't For Me

I know some of you may be beaming, thinking: "Lucky me. I don't have any credit card debt, so this book isn't for me." Wait a minute. Not so fast. Don't think for one second that you're immune, or that you couldn't get caught up in the debt woes that have ensnared so many others.

- *I don't care how much money you make.* It's not guaranteed.

- *I'm not impressed by your current high-powered position.* Even CEOs who built their own companies come and go; think of Martha Stewart.
- *Please don't tell me how secure your job is.* Let's get one thing straight. If you still believe in job security, I have a tooth fairy for you to meet and a bridge in Brooklyn to sell you.
- *It doesn't even matter how much cash you've invested in the stock market.* Investments rise and fall every day.

None of that matters if you haven't taken some basic precautions to safeguard yourself against personal emergencies that can easily become financial catastrophes. Want to know what sends people into the abyss of excessive debt? It can be anything from a lawsuit or legal judgment against a person to a business venture that went bust. Others with gambling addictions, alcohol-related problems, or drug dependencies often wind up in debt. All of these situations occur far too often – even if they don't represent the vast majority of those in debt.

Who Is In Debt and Why?

More often than not, people with heavy debt loads generally fit into two categories:
1) Over-spenders and poor money managers; and
2) Individuals who fall victim to "The Five Dreaded D's:"

- Divorce
- Downsizing
- Death
- Disability
- Disease

Have any "Dreaded D's" ever happened to you or someone you know? If so, you probably realize that any of these events can send one's finances into a tailspin.

So, before you think that all the debt-ridden people out there are just undisciplined, compulsive spenders, consider for a moment whether you could be right along with them: broke, unhappy with your circumstances, and in need of a solution.

After all, how would you be affected if you got divorced, lost your job, if the main breadwinner in your family died, if you became disabled and couldn't work, or if you or someone close to you suddenly took ill generating a pile of medical bills?

How Long Could You Last without Credit?

How long could you last without credit under dire circumstances? Could you keep up your current lifestyle without a paycheck, or manage your finances on a substantially reduced income? So remember, even if you don't owe a single dollar to a credit card company, you could ruin your finances by failing to shield yourself against financial disasters – disastrous *life events* that could ultimately drive you into debt. If you read on, though, I'll tell you how to protect yourself to help avoid such a scenario.

Take The Zero Debt Path to Financial Freedom

Everyone wants to achieve financial freedom. You can do it – regardless of your current situation.

Whether you're on the verge of filing for bankruptcy, you've paid off all your credit card debt but somehow don't quite have enough money to do whatever you'd like, or you're a high-wage earner who still frets over your finances, this book is for you. You can be free from financial worries. You can rest at night knowing not just that your bills are paid, that you've saved and invested wisely for the future, and that you have peace of mind when it comes to money matters, but that you've also laid the groundwork for your heirs to obtain financial freedom.

Take a minute and think about what financial freedom means for you.

Is it doing what you *want* to do for a living, instead of what you *have* to do? Is it finally seeing zero balances on all your credit cards? Is it enjoying a comfortable retirement in your Golden Years? Is it the ability to take exotic vacations, or even just travel to see friends in another city, without needing to penny pinch? Is it having enough money so that you can spend more time with your family?

Is it being able to leave an unsatisfying job – or perhaps kiss Corporate America goodbye altogether – and start your own business? Or maybe financial freedom to you means not having to work at all.

All of these things – and more – are possible when you become financially free. But the reality is that you can't have financial freedom if you're burdened with debt, anguishing over your bills, are living hand to mouth, aren't adequately saving, and have not protected whatever assets you do have.

That's where I come in – as your money coach. It's my mission to help get you financially fit.

I've written *Zero Debt* so that you can achieve your own personal definition of financial freedom. And whatever your definition may be, wouldn't it be great, in the not-too-distant future, to be able to declare with pride: "I'm totally, completely financially free!"

Believe it – because it's true. You can do it, starting with eliminating unnecessary or excessive debt. That's a huge step toward ridding yourself of financial worries.

Yes! You really *can* get on the road to financial freedom. And here's even better news: *you can do it yourself in the next 30 days.*

Want To Be Better Off a Month From Now?

Zero Debt won't give you one simple magic formula to make your debt completely disappear in a month's time. Nor will it teach you how to make a huge fortune in a few weeks. But it will reveal little-known secrets about what it takes to get long-lasting control of your finances – and manage your credit properly once and for all.

Having Excellent Credit – And "Good" Debt

For most individuals, getting credit isn't a problem; it's *managing* it that's the issue. Financial literacy is not widely taught at home or in school. So most of us muddle through the process of debt management: whether we're buying a vehicle, using a credit card, acquiring a house, or obtaining a student loan. Some people, however, refuse to pay for anything if they can't buy it all in cash. This approach may be a temporary fix that helps some people, but it's not generally a wise long-term strategy.

The truth of the matter is that we live in a credit-driven society. It's unrealistic, and in some cases detrimental to you, to simply say "I won't buy on credit" or "I will never use credit cards." You *need* credit for so many things – car rentals, purchasing a home, hotel stays, online purchases, etc. Moreover, having a strong credit profile can aid you in everything from getting an apartment, to securing the best life insurance rates, to landing a promotion on the job. So rather than suggesting that you run from credit, *Zero Debt* will help you embrace and harness the power derived from having good credit and solid debt management practices. Debt – in its proper form and used wisely – isn't something to be avoided, but leveraged.

Zero Debt will also be your blueprint for sound economic living and your roadmap to attaining wealth. You'll learn how to clean up your credit and increase your FICO® credit score; techniques to take the drudgery out of saving; what insurance you do (and don't) need; how to prevent identity theft; low-cost ways to create an updated will, and more. For those of you with serious debt problems, rest assured, there is hope for you too. I'm going to show you, step-by-step, exactly how to lay the foundation for your financial freedom. In the next 30 days, you'll get creditors off your back, learn creative ways to instantly put cash in your pocket, understand the real reasons you're overspending, and discover four ways to avoid blowing your budget. And that's just for starters.

I've Been Deep in Debt Too!

You see, I'm living proof that you can dig out of your debt hole. I know both sides of this issue first hand. In fact, I know what it's like to have $100,000 in credit card debt. That's not a typo … I meant what I said: *one hundred thousand dollars* in credit card debt! I also now know what it's like to be debt free. I currently own my own home, invest regularly in the stock market, have zero credit card debt, own a late-model car free and clear, and enjoy a comfortable lifestyle, complete with private school for the kiddies, timeshares, and regular vacations on the beach. If I could do it, so can you … if you implement the tips I share with you in *Zero Debt*.

Are you still too skeptical to give my advice a try? Well, what do you have to lose – besides your money worries or a ton of bills? Just one request: When you undergo the financial transformation that I know you will, be sure to visit my web site at www.themoneycoach.net and tell me about your success.

Now turn the page and let's get started … one day at a time.

Overview: We're A Nation of Debtors

If it's any consolation, you're not alone when it comes to having money problems or loads of bills. Collectively, consumers in the United States have racked up an unprecedented $2 trillion in personal debt, mainly from credit cards and auto loans. Here's what that means for you, someone you love, your next-door neighbor, or a colleague on the job:

- You probably feel like you're living paycheck to paycheck. *And you are.*
- You frequently find yourself worrying about money or bills.
- You aren't saving or investing enough for the future.
- You haven't protected whatever assets you do have.
- And within a decade, statistics show that one in 10 of you will file for bankruptcy.

Already, roughly 1.6 million American households seek bankruptcy protection each year. Why? Because the typical U.S. household has 13 cards – including debit, retail and credit cards. For those carrying a balance, the average credit card debt outstanding is roughly $13,000, and the average annual interest rate being paid on that debt is nearly 15%. Obviously, those with "bad" or "sub-prime" credit pay much more – more like 20% to 25%.

With $13,000 in debt, if you're making minimum payments on your cards, and paying 15% interest, it would take you more than 25 years to become debt free. And that's assuming you never charge another dime!

Generational Debt

It's well past time that we started addressing the scourge of chronic debt in America. Otherwise, we risk not just our own financial ruin – but also leaving a legacy of financial bondage for the next generation.

Guess who's the fastest-growing segment of the U.S. population filing for bankruptcy? Believe it or not, it's the folks who are *age 25 and under.* Young people are coming out of college with massive amounts of credit card debt, as well as student loans. College grads in the U.S. make about $52,000 annually – roughly twice the average annual income of non-graduates. But by and large, neither group of young adults has been taught about money management, so they primarily "inherit" their parents' spending habits and financial patterns. And what kind of example are most of us setting? Unfortunately, the majority of adults in this country aren't good financial role models.

The Warning Signs

Besides the alarming rate of bankruptcies, consider some of the other heinous tell tale signs of excessive debt in America:

- It's forcing people to literally work themselves to death.
- It's busting up marriages because couples are squabbling so much over money.
- It's preventing individuals from saving properly, and investing enough for their financial goals.
- It's pushing retirement back 5-10 years for those who are cash-strapped and carrying too much debt.
- It's robbing people of peace of mind and financial freedom.

Don't believe me? Well, the next time you visit a fast food restaurant, check out the growing number of elderly workers serving hamburgers and fries. Do you really think that they planned to spend their retirement slaving over a hot grill?

Consumer Debt On The Rise Internationally

Unfortunately, we've also exported our culture of debt globally. In decades past, credit-card use was not common at all in Europe. But that trend has changed dramatically in recent years. In 2004, the Bank of England reported that personal debt hit unprecedented levels – topping the $1.8 trillion mark. Debt from mortgages and credit cards now exceeds the U.K.'s annual national income from its production of goods and services. Like Americans, Britons have also been filing for bankruptcies at record rates. And experts forecast more households will go broke there and elsewhere. Hoyes, Michalos & Associates Inc. predicts that consumer bankruptcies in Canada will rise by 9% to 12% in 2004 and 2005. Those projections are based in part on several alarming statistics. As of 2003, Canadians carried debt equal to 104% of their disposable income, the highest level in history. And since 1977, Visa and MasterCard balances have increased annually by an average of 15.1%. The tide is also changing in Asia, where citizens are noted for being fastidious savers and have preferred cash to credit for generations. However, in places like South Korea and Hong Kong, credit card usage rates now mirror those of American consumers. The urge to splurge is even seen down under. Australians too are maxing out their credit cards, with the typical individual there owing a record $4,937 in personal debts, according to 2004 Reserve Bank figures.

A Few Words to Over-Spenders

Whether you're in London or Los Angeles, Toronto or Thailand, let me say a few words to those of you in the first category of debtors: the over-spenders and poor money managers.

You need to change what you've been doing. Period. If you don't, I can tell you unequivocally that you will never, ever have financial freedom. You will never experience the peace that comes from knowing that you don't have to deal with bounced checks, harassing phone calls from creditors, or the stress of constantly "robbing Peter to pay Paul."

Aren't you tired of wondering how you're going to make that next rent or mortgage payment? Isn't it mentally exhausting to have to figure out, month after month, how you'll scrape together money for basic necessities – like your light bill or phone service? Deep down, aren't you disgusted whenever you have put routine expenses, such as food, on a credit card because you don't have enough cash to pay for those purchases?

The Bling-Bling Lifestyle

Besides, what is all your spending for anyway? To keep up with the Joneses? To live a bling-bling lifestyle – or at least perpetrate the appearance of it? You're buying items you don't need (like designer shoes); wasting money on expensive cars and brand-name clothes you soon won't want; and salivating over today's "must have" things ... but they're things you won't even remember six months from now. I know, because I've been there.

Pull out your wallet or purse right now. Go ahead – it doesn't matter if you're at home, on your lunch break at work, or on an airplane. Take out all your credit cards and count them. How many do you have with you? Four? Eight? 12? And what about the ones at home? You know, the cards you put away because they're already maxed out, and you don't want the shame of getting declined again the next time you try to use them. It's time to move beyond those worries. It's time for you to obtain Zero Debt status, get smart about managing your money and your credit, and achieve financial freedom.

Where Did All Your Money Go?

If you keep it up, a year from now, three years from now, or whenever, you're going to look at your finances and ask yet again: "Where did all my money go?" or "What do I have to show for all my hard work?"

There could be a trigger event: Maybe you'll be getting married, so you and your prospective mate want to examine your finances. Maybe you'll experience a death in the family, and you'll realize that nothing is promised. Could be that you have or are expecting a baby, and now you're ready to get serious about your finances. Or perhaps you'll simply hit a certain age ... like 35, 50 or 65... whatever age gets you thinking about where you are and what you've accomplished thus far. Whatever trigger event happens, you're going to take stock of your life and wonder: "What in the world have I been doing with my money?"

Well, you don't have to wait. I can answer your question right now: What you've been doing is taking part in the craze of excessive consumerism that all of us – to greater or lesser degrees – have been seduced by. It's insanity. This cycle of wanting things, and spending more, then owing more, only to spend more and owe even more is outrageous. What you're doing to yourself – to your relationships, to your family—it's pure madness. To stop being a slave to debt, you've got to put a halt to this vicious, dead end, no-win cycle of excessive spending.

There is no other way. You've got to stop. Once and for all. Keep reading, and I'll show you how – one day at a time.

If you follow the Zero Debt Plan, I promise you that 30 days from now, you'll be infinitely better off than you are today. You'll feel better about your financial situation, you will have taken practical steps to protect your economic future, and you'll be able to see specific areas of progress where you've turned your finances around.

If you want to have Zero Debt and achieve financial freedom, you need a day-by-day plan to guide you to your destination. You must also know precisely what you need to *do* to get there.

This book is your plan. It's simple. It's easy to understand. And it works.

If It's So Simple, Why Doesn't Everyone Do It?

On paper, the process of reducing your debt as quickly as possible is actually fairly simple and straightforward. In basic terms, it really only requires three steps:

1. Stop digging (in other words, stop piling on additional debt).
2. Renegotiate your current debts (get your creditors to lower your interest or drop late fees).
3. Apply as much cash as you can toward your debt (by cutting back on expenses or generating additional income).

That's it. There's no magic formula. Simple -- right?

Well, reducing your debt may be *simple*, but it certainly isn't *easy*. That's why so many people remain buried under a mountain of debt. Additionally, there are numerous reasons you might be heavily indebted. So, depending on what threw you into debt, there could be many issues to address to dig yourself out of your financial hole.

Achieving true financial freedom also takes time, knowledge, and action – all based on the understanding that there has to be a better way to live a truly prosperous life. As a result, financial freedom always starts in the mind, not in your bank account. No one gets on the path to financial freedom without first *wanting* it and then *believing* it. Proverbs 23:7 says "As a man thinks, so he is." Put another way, the Bible teaches that a man *becomes* what he *practices* – in thoughts, words, and actions. From now on, you have to have *faith* that your money problems can become a thing of the past. And for most of us, that usually only happens *after* you've had your fair share of financial troubles.

But more than anything, becoming financially free requires a plan. And most people just don't have one.

Starting today, though, *you* will.

As your money coach, I'll tell you how to approach eliminating your debt, what steps to take and in which order. I'll lead you by the hand through your first 30 days, and after that – well, after that the rest is up to you.

All The Motivation You Need

How motivated are you to turn your life around? No, let me rephrase that question: How angry are you that you're not where you want to be, where you *should* be at your age?

You should be angry at your current circumstances. Actually, you should be *really* ticked off. Take that righteous indignation and use it constructively. I'm counting on that anger, because I intend to teach you to take what each of you already has – a burning desire to be free from money worries, and a willingness to learn – and use those things to your advantage. Use what you're feeling now to help cast a vision for yourself, an image of where you'd like to be when you get out of your debt dilemma. Hold that picture in your mind as you read *Zero Debt*.

Before we get started with the day-by-day steps to slash your debt, there's one other thing you should know.

Diagnosis: You're Suffering From The Debt Disease

I have to reveal a personal bias of mine when it comes to credit card debt. I feel strongly that excessive debt is the worst possible financial cancer you can have. In fact, I believe that debt for many people is a byproduct of a terrible disease – an insidious malady known as consumerism – and as a symptom of a disease, debt should be treated as such.

If you think about it, many aspects of chronic spending, and the debt that results from it, are really no different than alcoholism. Check out the following 10 similarities.

Excessive consumerism and alcoholism both:

1. Generate stress and physical illness (migraines, ulcers, etc. can result from money worries)

2. Tear families apart (70% of all couples that divorce cite financial strife as a major problem in their marriage)

3. Produce short-term euphoria or escapism from daily problems

4. Can be generational (Don't you know people whose behavior just mimics what their mom or dad did?)

5. Make individuals feel shame, guilt and embarrassment

6. Have complex underlying or root causes for the behavior

7. Cause victims to feel out of control with their actions

8. Produce hangovers (for the alcoholic, a drinking binge leads to a physical hangover; for the shopaholic, a spending binge creates a debt hangover that lasts months or years)

9. May require individuals to change their habits, their friends, the places they frequent, etc. to reduce temptations

10. Have similar and predictable phases of deterioration:

  - Denial

The phase where the person refuses to admit he/she has a problem, as in: "I don't have too much debt," "I don't shop too much" or perhaps: "I can handle my bills."

  - Worsening of the problem

When the debts mount, late fees occur, bill collectors call, etc.

  - Hitting 'rock bottom'

Characterized by traumatic financial events, such as foreclosure, bankruptcy, personal or business lawsuits, and so forth.

- Intervention

Sometimes the intervention is from within the family, as when a husband takes away his wife's credit cards. Other times, the intervention/help comes from an external source, such as when a person voluntarily goes to a debt management program.

Now that you can see the common areas between excessive consumerism and alcoholism, is it any wonder that debt has such a stranglehold over you?

But don't despair. You don't have to remain drunk with debt. You can kick your spending addiction, if that is what has put you in this mess. Each of you can break the cycle of debt. With the right know-how and some positive action, you truly can fix your finances once and for all.

Again, it won't be easy. But I'm going to ask you to exercise a little faith – and a lot of *follow through*. In other words, don't just *read* this book. Over the next 30 days, put my recommendations into practice. Do what I'm telling you to do and see if your financial picture doesn't begin to drastically improve.

O.K. … I know you're excited and ready now for the exact steps you need to take to begin turning your financial life around. Here they are …

Week Number 1

This week you will:

- Stop the flood of credit card offers you get
- Resolve to "stop digging" deeper into debt
- Put down everything you owe in writing
- Order your credit report and FICO® score
- Negotiate with your creditors to save money
- Switch credit cards if necessary
- Exceed your minimum payments due

Day 1 Stop the flood of credit card offers.

Ever notice how your mailbox seems to be flooded with credit card offers every week? If your residence is like the average U.S. household, you probably get dozens of credit card solicitations in the mail each year. To put an end to them, simply call 888-5-OPT-OUT. This will force the credit bureaus to stop selling your name and address to banks and other institutions that send you credit card offers each month.

The Consumer Federation of America (CFA) in Washington D.C. tracks the rate at which banks and other credit card issuers send out credit card offers. What CFA discovered is that some five billion credit card solicitations were sent out in 2001 … Imagine that, five billion credit card offers, or 50 per U.S. household! According to Synovate, a Chicago-based research company, the numbers dropped slightly to 4.89 billion credit offers mailed in 2002 and 4.29 billion in 2003. Still, that's an awful lot of plastic being dangled before the public. Synovate's "Mail Monitor" report also found that 90% of credit card mail comes from the 10 largest credit card issuers.

Critics say that credit card companies are too aggressive in their marketing, often lure consumers with 0% offers or short-term teaser rates, and are quick to impose late fees, penalties or other unfavorable terms for the slightest misstep by consumers.

Interestingly, though, consumers are saying a resounding "No" to credit card companies, according to CFA, Synovate and other industry sources. More often than not, people are tearing up those credit card applications or saying "thanks, but no thanks" to the telemarketers who call to offer new credit. For all the mail being sent out, direct mail doesn't seem to be the most profitable way for credit card companies to do business. For starters, they have to send out about 200 solicitations just to acquire one new customer. That means roughly $120 spent to attract every new cardholder because response rates are very low ... just 0.6%, according to the most recent figures available from Synovate.

Trends In Credit Card Marketing

Even though this "thumbs down to new credit" trend is going on, credit card companies are finding other ways to win business. Some are focusing their efforts on keeping the clients they already have, and trying to keep consumers loyal to a particular brand. Other companies are emphasizing card benefits such as airlines miles or shopping-rewards programs, and are slowly backing away from blanketing consumers with balance transfer options and 0% deals. These companies have found that when 0% offers end, many consumers simply card hop, and go find another 0% offer.

The Consumer Federation of America highlights another tactic. It says that some credit card companies are raising the limits that are being offered to consumers. So in the past, if you might've received an offer for a Visa with a $5,000 credit line, now you're apt to get one with a $10,000 credit line. From the CFA's point of view, this is a way that credit card companies try to entice you, by making a sweeter offer that they hope you won't be able to refuse.

A Sweeter Offer?

I recall very clearly a time when I was up to my eyeballs in debt, but had just paid off one credit card in full. Suddenly, a barrage of new credit card offers appeared in my mailbox. One of them was a card with a pre-approved $20,000 credit line. Was it tempting? Only for about two seconds. I declined the offer. But I saved the form to remind myself that credit card issuers were never going to stop tempting me. It was up to me – and me alone – to exercise restraint if I wanted to pay down my debts, and properly manage my credit.

The Truth About Credit Card Companies

In fairness, I have to say two things in defense of the credit card companies. First of all, believe it or not, they really don't want you to become so indebted that you can't pay your bills. I know that a lot of you mistakenly think that credit card companies love it when you're behind on your payments because then they can jack up the interest rate. After all, they're in business to make money. And one way they do that is by collecting interest charges on purchases you and I make. But creditors are also aware of the possibility that if things get really bad for you, you have the option to file for bankruptcy protection, which (at least under current law) would give you the right to wipe out your credit card debt entirely. So trust me, they really don't want you to sink into a financial hole.

Are You Playing The Blame Game?

Additionally, every consumer has to take some level of personal accountability for his or her actions. The truth of the matter is that even with all the billions of credit card offers being extended each year, no one is putting a gun to your head and making you say "Yes."

Are all those offers tempting? Sure they are. But the credit card company alone can't be held solely responsible for your decision to say "Yes" any more than the restaurant waitress who comes after dinner with a cart full of delicious cakes, mouth-watering pies, and tantalizing chocolates, and asks: "Dessert anyone?"

Is she to be blamed for your ever-expanding waistline if you say "Yes" to dessert every month when you patronize that restaurant? Of course not. Well, by the same token, your ever-growing credit card debt is not entirely the credit card company's fault if you choose to "bite" at their credit card offers and then find yourself in financial trouble.

What's the solution? If you don't have the restraint right now to say "No," and you haven't yet learned to properly manage your credit or spending, do yourself a favor and opt out of most credit card offers by calling 888-5-OPT-OUT. Right now, you just don't need that temptation.

One Easy Phone Call Can Help

The toll-free number I've given you, 888-5-OPT-OUT is an automatic phone service that's run by the four main credit reporting agencies: TransUnion, Experian, Equifax, and Innovis. (Many of you may be thinking: "What is Innovis?" I'll tell you more about that company – and the credit report you've probably never even heard of – later, in **Day 4**. For now, though, let's stay with this OPT-OUT number).

The reason this number works is because it takes you out of the credit bureaus' databases for pre-screened mailings. When you're ready to take your name off these marketing lists, follow these instructions:

Step 1. Call 1-888-5-OPT-OUT (888-567-8688)
Step 2. Select Option 2 to skip the message about an Internet email.
Step 3. Select Option 2 to opt out of mailings permanently. (Don't choose Option 1, because that will only opt you out for two years.)
Step 4. Follow the directions to enter your correct telephone number, address, name, and social security number.

The recording will tell you that the information you enter is confidential and will only be used to remove your name from the list. After you're done providing your personal information, you will get a message from this service advising you that your request will be handled within five business days. The recorded message will also state that a "Notice of Election" form will be mailed to your address. This form simply confirms that you have chosen to opt of out receiving credit card offers. Be aware, though, that you may still get some credit card offers in the mail. How so? These offers may come from any credit-granting companies that do not use these credit card companies to secure their list of pre-screened consumers.

Finally, if you have other people in your household who want to opt out, the 888-5-OPT-OUT service also gives you the option to leave information for an additional family member. To do so, select Option 1 at the end of the message when prompted.

Opting Out By Mail

If you don't want to use the phone, you can also write to each one of the credit bureaus and request that your name be removed from their pre-screened lists. In your letter, state clearly that you want to "opt out" of credit card offers. Be sure to provide the credit agency with your name, mailing address, city, zip and social security number. If you've moved within the past six months, don't forget to also include your old address.

End All – Well, At Least Most – Junk Mail

While you're at it, if you really want to stem the tide of junk mail you're getting – not just credit cards – but all solicitations, you may want to consider writing to the Direct Marketing Association. Tell this group that you'd like to add your name to their Mail Preference Service. When you register for this service, your name and address are placed on a "do not mail" list." All DMA members must check their list of potential customers against the "do not mail" file. So if your name is on that list, the marketing company must remove you from its mailings. To get registered as soon as possible, you'll have to pay $5 and register online. In return, you'll get about 95% less junk mail for five years. You can also get on the Mail Preference Service list free of charge, by writing The Direct Marketing Association. This is a slower process, but it works.

The Direct Marketing Association reports that its "do not mail" file is updated each month and distributed four times a year: in January, April, July and October. The organization says you usually see a drop in the amount of mail you receive about three months after registering for their service. Again, it's faster if you use their online registration process. Also, if you move, you have to register your new address with the Mail Preference Service to make sure marketers don't send you unwanted mail.

Here's how to reach The Direct Marketing Association:

Mail Preference Service
ATTN: DEPT. 13586375
Direct Marketing Association
P.O. Box 282
Carmel, NY 10512
http://www.the-dma.org

Remember: not all companies use the DMA Mail Preference Service to purge their mailing lists. So it's possible [likely, in fact], that you will still get some companies' promotions. When this happens, just contact the company directly and request that your name and address be placed on the company's "do not mail" list.

Day 2 Make a resolution to "stop digging."

Famed billionaire investor Warren Buffett once said that if you find yourself in a hole, the first thing you must do is to "stop digging." It may sound basic, but every day, people with massive amounts of consumer debt continue to dig themselves deeper into the red by spending as if there's no tomorrow. If you *know* you've been over-spending, you must vow to end negative spending habits. This is *crucial* to fixing your finances. Let me put it another way: if you're serious about chucking your credit card debt, you have to put an end to frivolous or excessive spending – starting today!

So many of us tend to make empty promises to ourselves and others: promises that we'll spend less and save more; promises that next year we'll get our act together; promises that with the next promotion or the next bonus or the next money that comes in we'll make good use of that cash – anything related to whipping our finances into shape. It especially happens at the beginning of the year. Have you ever made a New Year's resolution concerning your finances? More to the point, if you have such a resolution going forward, chances are you'll need all the help you can get to stay on track. The December holiday season is the time of year that many of us tend to overspend – leaving you with big credit card bills, and the equivalent of a shopper's hangover that lasts well into the following year.

For those of you determined to better manage your money, you don't have to live a life of deprivation in order to get into the black. The best way to turn your financial resolutions into lasting changes is to take some concrete steps that won't cramp your style, but will definitely improve your personal finances.

Here are some ways you can do just that.

- **Create a realistic financial plan.**

A proper financial plan provides you with a snapshot of where you are today – in terms of assets and liabilities, and your current cash flow. It also outlines your short, medium and long-term goals, such as saving for a down payment on a house or taking a dream vacation. Finally, a well-crafted financial plan should include a number of "must do" items, like you must start contributing to your IRA or you must pay off your Visa bill.

Don't make the mistake of thinking "If only I could stay out of the mall, I could get my finances under control." Staying out of the mall may be necessary for you die-hard shoppers who need to change their surroundings and avoid too much temptation. But getting your finances in order is not necessarily, and certainly not exclusively, about will power. It's about creating such an awesome plan of action that you don't want to deviate from it because you can clearly see all the benefits of having a financially sound household. After all, which of the following circumstances are most appealing? Scenario #1, in which you and your spouse are always bickering about money and you have to live paycheck to paycheck, or Scenario #2, in which you've lived within your means and your money squabbles all but disappear? When you need motivation, remember that by sticking to your resolutions, especially your newly-created financial plan, you'll not only save yourself big bucks, you'll ultimately have financial freedom, and far less worries and stress about money.

- **Make this money resolution**: "Before I buy something, I will think about *why* I'm spending. I will spend money only for the *right* reasons."

Why We Spend

We all dole out cash for things we *need*, such as food, clothing and shelter. But we also buy plenty of things just because we *want* them or because we feel: "*I deserve it*." After all, we all work hard for our money. So what's the big deal about splurging every once in a while, right? Well, the big deal is that if you're serious about getting out of a financial pit, your splurging days are over – at least for now.

You must also be careful of spending solely *to impress* others, like buying luxury cars or fancy jewelry just for show. Think about that for a minute. How many people do you know really just spend to show off the latest, the so-called best, or the most fashionable this or that? What good is having a Lexus or a Mercedes if you're still renting and don't own your own home? And whom are you really kidding if you're buying Gucci and Prada, yet you still worry about your credit card getting declined?

Other times, people spend simply because they're angry, depressed or bored. Maybe you just had an argument with your man – and ladies you know if I'm talking to you – and because he ticked you off, all of a sudden you're in the mall. Or perhaps a boss is frustrating you on the job, or a co-worker is getting on your nerves.

So what do you do? You start spending as a temporary, quick fix *to feel better*. Try your best to avoid "retail therapy." That's when you start purchasing cosmetics or an expensive new pair of shoes (even though you have tons of each at home) in an effort to give yourself an emotional pick-me-up.

Make a point to avoid spending *out of habit* too. Many of us literally spend money on habits – things like cigarettes or alcohol. If you've got such a habit, realize that it could be costing you your fiscal and physical health. Even those habitual patterns that aren't detrimental to our bodies, might still be harmful to our bank accounts. For instance, I know many women who go to the hair salon, or get regular manicures and pedicures mainly out of habit. They've always done it, it's routine to them, and practically nothing on God's green earth is going to stop them from hitting the salons week after week after week.

Now don't get me wrong. I like to look as nice and as put together as the next woman. But my point is that if you're struggling to pay your bills, can you really afford to fork over $50 a week (or whatever you might be paying) for the luxury of "beautifying" yourself? Personally, I don't think it's really worth it to look the part of "the fabulous diva" on the outside, when on the inside you're stressed out and feeling more like "the fake debtor" because everybody thinks you've got it all together, but deep down, you know the scary truth about your situation.

There's one other point about this subject that is worth addressing, in case you're thinking: "Honey, getting my hair and nails done, that's not a *luxury*; it's a *necessity*!" I'd like you to at least *consider* another perspective about certain things that we

41

spend money on. Read the advice contained in **Day 16** for some insights about the ways in which we surrender our money on things that *we* might think are "necessities," but *others* consider "luxuries," "frivolous," or "downright wasteful."

By now some of you may be thinking: Darn! Is there anything I *can* spend on? And the answer is: Of course there is. Obviously you should feel free to spend money on the things you need. No one is suggesting that you walk around unclothed, without proper shelter or hungry. People will often say, "Lynnette, I also *need* a car – I have to get to work." To which I answer, "Yes, you need a car, but does it really have to be a *brand new* one or a $50,000 vehicle?" Just live within your means and be reasonable in your spending – even when buying the things you *need*.

You can, and also should, spend *to help* others -- i.e. to aid your family, church or a favorite charity -- when you can afford to do so. And it's even OK to open your wallet to buy, have or do what you *want* (think art lessons, graduate school or travel) in order *to improve* your quality of life or invest in yourself or family members.

But I've discovered that a lot of us spend for the wrong reasons. Sometimes people spend to exert power and control over others: like when parents tell their high school or college-age children: "I'll buy you XYZ, but only if you do what I say, or go to the school I choose," etc. Men (and women) have also been known to use money as a way to keep their significant others in check; or they buy them gifts in a misguided effort to secure the other party's love and affection – or even to get out of the doghouse after an argument or some exhibition of "bad" behavior. All of this crazy spending must cease immediately.

Wage War On Your Debt

You've heard of "Cease Fire" agreements when nations are at war, right? Well, right now consider yourself at war with your debt. It's a battle you'll win if you start off with a "take no prisoners" attitude. And that means beginning with the mindset that NO MATTER WHAT you will not spend beyond your means, you will not spend for the wrong reasons, and you will no longer pile on additional credit card debt. Instead of a "Cease Fire" agreement, you're now going to create a "Cease Spending" pact with yourself.

- **Write out your very own *"Declaration to Achieve Zero Debt."*** Use the following model as your guide.

I, insert your name here, *realize that I am in a financial hole. Therefore, I hereby vow to stop digging myself further into debt. I acknowledge that I can never be free from money worries if I continue to spend excessively, for the wrong reasons, or on unnecessary things. From this day forward* (insert month date and year) *I will be more conscious of my spending habits, being careful to keep my behavior in line with my desire to reduce my debt and achieve financial freedom.*

Get this statement free at www.themoneycoach.net. Print it and insert your name and date. Then put it in a visible place as a reminder of your commitment to financially empower yourself.

Day 3 Put all your debts in writing.

Today you're going to write down everything you owe your creditors. That's right, *everything* – from your student loans, to mortgages, to credit card debt, medical bills, auto loans, etc.

On a piece of paper, make a complete list of your obligations and here's what you should write or type out on the sheet: Include the name and phone number of each creditor, your account number, the interest rate you pay, the total balance due, and the minimum monthly payment.

Why Torture Yourself Listing All Your Bills?

You need this information in black and white to get a realistic picture of where you are. This info will also help you later when it's time to negotiate with creditors or collection agencies. Again, write down *everything* that you owe, even including credit cards that might have only $100 on them. Don't make the mistake of leaving those "small" bills out because "Oh, I'm going to pay that one off this month anyway." Just write down everything you actually owe as of today.

Many people have a rough idea about how much they owe their creditors. But there's no substitute for having true, accurate numbers – not guesstimates. To fill in the proper figures on your written sheet, or your computer spreadsheet, you'll have to go find your most recent statements and invoices from your creditors. Take as much time as you need today to collect all this data. It's a crucial step in you getting your finances together.

It's also a good idea to call the companies you owe and ask for the latest information about your debt, especially if you're looking at statements that are more than a month old. Even if the statements are current, you should call your creditors because some of the information on those statements may have changed. For instance, you may have charged additional items since the closing date on your credit card statement, so now your debt is actually greater than your current statement indicates. Also, you may have had a teaser rate or a lower interest rate in the past, and maybe that interest rate has now jumped. Whatever the case, you need to have the most accurate information that is currently available.

A Wake-Up Call: How Much Do You Owe?

The next step is for you to add up all your debts. For some of you, seeing your total debt in black and white may be a scary thing: a wake up call to how deeply you are in financial bondage. For others, seeing your total debt may offer relief: perhaps you don't owe as much as you feared.

Whatever the situation, don't panic. Remember, you're on the path to financial freedom now and if your goal is to get to "Zero Debt" status, keep plugging along – it will happen, and sooner than you think!

I Debticate Myself to Being Debt-Free

If you need a little help to get your list of creditors down on paper, use this handy form on the next page that I've created, called "I **Debt**icate Myself to Being Debt-Free." It's meant to give you an honest, black-and-white look at where you are today. Later, the form will also serve as an incentive when you're slashing your debts one at a time. You can download a copy of this form from www.themoneycoach.net, and then fill it in appropriately. You'll find this document under the "Free Info" area. Just click on the PDF that says "I **Debt**icate Myself to Being Debt **Free**." Don't skip this step – do it today! At the very least, answer this question now: How many credit cards are in your wallet? A wallet full of plastic, especially charge cards that are at their limit, is definitely a sign that you're carrying too much debt.

I Debticate Myself To Being **Debt-Free**

Creditor	Account Number	Phone Number	Interest Rate	Balance Due	Minimum Monthly Payment
1.					
2.					
3.					
4.					
5.					
6.					
7.					
8.					
9.					
10.					
11.					
12.					
13.					
14.					
15.					

Copyright Lynnette Khalfani   www.themoneycoach.net

Day 4 Order your credit report and FICO® score.

Visit www.myfico.com to get your FICO® credit score and your credit report instantly online for a fee. This site has your individual credit reports from Equifax, Experian, and Trans Union – and for each credit bureau report you buy, myFICO gives you an individual FICO® credit score. At last check, the cost of obtaining the three credit reports and your FICO® credit score at www.myfico.com was $38.85. I do recommend buying all three reports as sometimes one agency's credit report may list certain accounts or information about you that is not contained in the other credit bureaus' reports. And you obviously want the most comprehensive information contained in your credit files.

What is a FICO® Score?

For those of you who are unfamiliar with credit scores, you should know that practically all lenders use credit scores. Some 75% of all mortgages lenders use FICO® scores and 98% of the top 50 credit card companies use FICO® scores to determine whether or not to grant consumers loans, making FICO® scores the most popularly used credit scores in the country. FICO® stands for Fair Isaac Corporation. That's the Minneapolis-based firm that developed the credit scoring software used to assess your credit-worthiness. In short, banks and other financial institutions look at your credit score to determine whether or not to extend to you a mortgage, an auto loan, credit cards, and so forth. FICO® scores range from 300 to 850. The higher your score, the better a credit risk you are deemed. Translation: the higher your score, the more likely it is statistically that you will pay your debts on time. Therefore, those with better scores save money because banks will make lower interest loans to those consumers than to others with less-than-stellar credit records.

For instance, look at the difference in borrowing costs for anyone getting a $150,000 fixed rate, 30-year mortgage:

FICO® Score	Your Interest Rate	Your Mo. Payment
720-850	6.13%	$912
700-719	6.25%	$924
675-699	6.79%	$977
620-674	7.94%	$1,094
560-619	8.53%	$1,157
500-559	9.29%	$1,238

Source: myFICO.com as of July 2004

As you can see from this example, a borrower with top-level credit would pay $326 a month less than a consumer at the bottom rung of the credit ladder. That's an annual savings of $3,912 dollars, no small chunk of change. And when you think about that savings magnified over 30 years – to the tune of more than $117,000 – it's clear that it pays to protect your credit.

While you can call a credit-reporting agency, such as TransUnion and get your credit report, I think the best thing for consumers to do is to use www.myfico.com. Here's why: Not only will you learn what information is contained in your credit report, but you'll also get specific recommendations – straight from the horse's mouth, so to speak – on what specific steps you can take to improve your FICO® score over time. Plus, you'll learn how to *use* your credit score; and it's here where the www.myfico.com site is a most valuable resource.

At www.myfico.com, you'll find loads of information that tells you how to leverage your FICO® score to full advantage by shopping around for the best-rate loans. There are plenty of pointers on how to improve your credit standing, data about how lenders view consumers with similar credit profiles to yours, and even tips on how to guard your credit by thwarting identity theft. FICO® also offers an insightful, free 17-page guide online called "Understanding Your Credit Score."

Additionally, the FICO® score simulator – available online after you purchase your credit report – is a handy tool that lets you see the impact of certain actions on your credit score. For instance, using the FICO® score simulator, you can see how your credit score might improve (or worsen) if you do things like pay off all your debts, or (heaven forbid) miss a payment in the future.

Finally, if you can't afford to purchase your credit report from Fair Isaac – or any company for that matter – the www.myfico.com site gives you free access to the FICO® score estimator. You answer 10 questions online and then Fair Isaac gives you its best determination, within a given range, of what your

FICO® score is likely to be. At least this gives you an idea of where you stand.

If you don't have Internet access to get your credit report and FICO® score, or if you prefer to deal directly with the credit agencies, call Equifax at 800-685-1111; Experian at 888-397-3742 and TransUnion at 800-916-8800. Mailing addresses for these credit bureaus, as well as Innovis, are in Appendix A. (Read about Innovis at the end of this chapter. What you'll learn may shock you).

Now that you have some background information about why you should get your credit report and FICO® score, let's talk about some of the biggest misconceptions regarding credit scores. As a consumer, your credit is of such critical importance that you can't afford to operate on the basis of false information. For starters, realize that you do have the power to upgrade your credit profile. "Your credit score is something you can improve – with time and discipline," says Fair Isaac spokesman Ryan Sjoblad. The following section tells you the real truth about credit scores.

Fact Vs. Fiction About Credit Scores

FICTION: If I check my credit report often, all those "inquiries" will lower my credit score.

FACT: Your personal inquiries are called "soft" inquiries and do not impact your credit score at all. You can check your credit as much as you'd like with no negative impact, as long as you do it through a credit bureau or a company authorized to issue credit reports, such as myFICO.

EXPLANATION: Even though you may see all kinds of inquiries in your credit file, many of them have no bearing on your FICO® score. For instance, your FICO® score doesn't count your own inquiries, as well as those from existing creditors who are reviewing your account, or lenders trying to offer you "pre-approved" credit.

FICTION: I pay cash for everything and don't buy on credit or use credit cards, so my credit score should be excellent.

FACT: Having no credit history or never using credit can have a negative impact on your credit score.

EXPLANATION: It helps your FICO® score to have some history of paying credit obligations on time. Fair Isaac reports that people with no credit cards tend to be higher risk than those who have managed their debts responsibly.

FICTION: I'm going to close out my old accounts since I'm not using them any more, and that will improve my credit score.

FACT: You can actually hurt your credit score by closing older, more "seasoned" accounts.

EXPLANATION: Generally speaking, it works in your favor to have older accounts in your credit file because it shows that you have a longer credit history.

FICTION: The most important factor in my credit score is whether or not I am "maxed out" on my credit cards.

FACT: The single biggest determinant of your credit score is how well you've paid your bills on time in the past.

EXPLANATION: Your FICO® score takes into account whether or not you've had late or missed payments, how far past due your bills were, how long ago the late pays occurred, and whether you have any collection items.

FICTION: My age, race, gender, marital status, income or where I live can impact my credit score.

FACT: None of those factors are taken into consideration at all when your FICO® credit score is determined.

EXPLANATION: Under U.S. law, it is illegal to for credit scoring to take into account race, age, color, nationality, religion, sex and marital status.

Because there is so much misinformation about what goes into your credit score, I thought you'd like to know directly from Fair Isaac how the company comes up with your FICO® score. In short, your credit file is reviewed and certain information about how you've managed your credit is statistically analyzed. Ultimately, five different categories are weighted to produce your FICO® score. Here's the breakdown of those five areas that contribute to your FICO® score:

What a FICO® Score Considers

1. **Payment History:** Approximately 35% of your score is based on this category.

2. **Amounts Owed:** About 30% of your score is based on this category.

3. **Length of Credit History:** Roughly 15% of your score is based on this category.

4. **New Credit:** Around 10% of your score is based on this category.

5. **Types of Credit in Use:** About 10% of your credit score is based on this category.

Is Credit Scoring Fair To Minorities?

Critics oppose credit scoring for two reasons. First, some argue that so much data collection intrudes on people's privacy. Also, some critics say that credit scoring discriminates against minorities. Fair Isaac officials dispute both assertions, especially the concept that credit scoring is unfair to minorities.

"Gender, race and nationality are factors that do not get added into the FICO scores," says Fair Isaac spokesman Ryan Sjoblad. "It knows nothing about you, except your credit-paying habits. It's hard to call it (credit scoring) racist, when it has no idea what your race is."

Little-Known Ways Your Credit Impacts You

Most people know that a poor credit score can impact your ability to get a mortgage, car, and credit cards. But did you know that your credit history has a much wider-ranging impact on you, far beyond your ability to obtain credit or loans?

"A lot of things are based on trust and your credit report, to some degree, talks about how trustworthy you are," says Eric

Simons, a certified financial planner and head of Simons Financial Network in New York.

According to Simons and other experts, your credit history can also be legally considered if you're applying for automobile, medical or life insurance, are trying to rent a new apartment, or are seeking a new job or even a promotion at your existing place of employment.

Say you are up for a better-paying position at your company, one that would require you to manage a budget or deal with customer funds. Under the law, your bosses are entitled to check out your credit history as part of their evaluation of you – as long as they do it in accordance with the Fair Credit Reporting Act.

What this means is that they must first get your permission to check your credit. They must also inform you of your rights under the law. These rights include the right to dispute the accuracy or completeness of any information supplied by a credit reporting agency, and the right to a free consumer report upon request within 60 days. Also, if any of the information your employer obtains causes them to deny you a promotion or act "adversely" toward you, they must notify you in writing of which credit reporting agency they used.

The same notification requirements hold true for any insurance company that decides to terminate your policy, deny you insurance, or increase your rates if such adverse action in taken based solely or partially on information in your consumer report.

Check out a couple of news items recently about the links between insurance and credit:

- In Alaska: lawmakers were considering legislation that would halt credit scoring after receiving complaints that bad drivers with good credit paid lower car insurance rates than others who had good driving records but poor credit
- In Washington: authorities have started limiting the extent to which companies can use people's credit histories to determine whether to issue new policies, and renew or cancel existing ones

The "Big Three" Credit Bureaus

If you have blemishes on your credit record, you may want to submit a letter to the three main credit bureaus – Experian, Equifax and Trans Union – that succinctly explains why certain derogatory information may appear on your credit report. "It's a beautiful way to show your side of the story, right up front, proactively," says Simons, the certified financial planner.

"Give a quick, non bleeding heart explanation about what has happened, why it happened and why it won't happen again," he recommends. "This makes you a better-looking prospective borrower."

Finally, you should take some time to read up on and learn about a handful of other important rights under the Fair Credit Reporting Act (FCRA). You'll find more details about the FCRA in **Day 8** of *Zero Debt*. But briefly, among these rights granted to consumers are the following:

- You can dispute inaccurate information contained in your file.

Once you tell a consumer-reporting agency that something in your file is wrong, that agency must investigate the item in dispute, typically within 30 days. Ultimately, the credit agency must give you a written report summarizing the investigation. It must also provide you with an updated copy of your credit report if their investigation changes your report.

- Erroneous information must be corrected or deleted.

But if something is correct, that data doesn't have to be removed unless it's outdated or can't be verified.

- Only businesses with legitimate purposes can view your credit report – and then only with your permission.

For instance, in considering your application, a creditor, employer, landlord, insurer, or other such legitimate businesses can obtain information about you from a consumer-reporting agency.

Are You Eligible For a Free Credit Report?

If you ever get turned down for credit, you are automatically entitled to a free credit report under the Equal Credit Opportunity Act. Just make your request to the credit bureaus within 60 days of being denied credit. Also, anyone who is very poor (or considered "indigent"), victims of identity theft, and those who are unemployed are legally entitled to a free credit report under federal law.

Moreover, if you happen to live in Colorado, Connecticut, Georgia, Maine, Maryland, Massachusetts, New Jersey or Vermont, you lucked out. Residents in these eight states are entitled to one free credit report annually from each of the three primary credit bureaus.

The Credit Report You've Probably Never Heard Of

I just mentioned how you can get a copy of your credit file from one of the "Big 3" credit-reporting agencies. But did you know that there's a fourth credit bureau of considerable influence in this country?

The company is called Innovis, and if you're smart, you'll definitely want to also contact Innovis and find out what information this company is reporting about you.

As recently as 2003, Innovis denied that it was actually in the credit-reporting business. There are numerous published reports in which the company flat-out denied that the information it gathers or sells about consumers could be used by creditors for the purpose of extending credit. The company's tight-lipped policies caused NBC to warn consumers that "Innovis is a secret credit bureau that sells your credit information to companies that compile mailing lists for unsolicited mail, including charge cards."

Shortly thereafter, consumer advocates – like the Public Interest Research Group (PIRG) – starting insisting that Innovis was in fact a credit bureau and should have to abide by the same rules as other credit agencies. After some outside pressure and scrutiny,

Innovis now acknowledges that it is, indeed a credit reporting agency.

According to published reports, Innovis primarily collects negative information about consumers: things like late payments, judgments, bankruptcies, collection accounts, repossessions, and so forth. That information is then sold to banks and other financial institutions. Remember in **Day 1** when I advised you to stop the flood of credit offers coming to your home? Well, if you *do* get credit offers, you certainly want them to be the best ones available, like low interest rate balance transfers, for instance.

But when companies buy data from Innovis, reportedly what they are screening for is people with "bad" credit – or at least people who *used* to have bad credit. This can have two effects on you. First, it would screen you out of the lists of top-tier consumers who are getting low-interest credit offers. Second, it makes you open game for getting a host of credit offers you probably don't want to get. Think about it for a minute: If a bank or credit card company is actively targeting consumers with poor credit histories, what kind of credit offers do you think they'll be making? More than likely, they'll be throwing out high interest-rate offers – above the 20% level – or solicitations for "secured" credit cards. Again if you're already considered a "sub-prime" borrower, you don't want to get these offers. So make sure you write Innovis and find out what information the company has about you.

Unlike the other credit bureaus – that let you get your credit report online or talk to representatives over the telephone, Innovis doesn't make it easy to establish contact. The only way you can obtain your Innovis credit report is by writing the company. You'll find Innovis's mailing address in Appendix A of *Zero Debt*. The company's 800-number is also listed. But when you call, it's just a recorded information line telling you to put your request in writing.

To get your Innovis credit report, send them a letter asking for your credit file. Be sure to include your name, current address, and social security number. Innovis also requires your previous address for the last two years if you haven't been at your current residence for two years, your date of birth, a copy of your driver's license or a utility bill to verify your address, your telephone number, your current employer, and your signature.

The fee for obtaining your credit report from Innovis varies from $3 to $9, depending on your state of residence. One bit of good news: individuals living in the eight states mentioned above – CO, CT, GA, ME, MD, MA, NJ and VT – can get a free credit report from Innovis, just as they can from the "Big Three" credit bureaus.

When you get your credit reports, if you see any bills or accounts that you left off the list of debts you created in **Day 3**, go ahead and add those debts to your list now. And just remember: the single-best thing you can do from this day forward to boost your credit standing is to *pay your bills on time.*

Day 5 Call your creditors & negotiate.

Many people deep in debt may feel powerless to change their situation in terms of getting their creditors to give them a break. But nothing could be further from the truth. Under the right circumstances, and armed with the right knowledge, you can win concessions from banks, credit card companies and other s that you owe.

Your next step now is to use the list you created in **Day 3**, and contact each creditor and ask for a lower interest rate. Depending on how much debt you have, doing this one step alone can save you hundreds, if not thousands of dollars – not to mention shave many months or years off the time you'll be paying off your debt.

You Have Leverage

Don't make the mistake of thinking that just because you owe money you don't have any power when it comes to dealing with credit card companies. The truth of the matter is you probably have far more leverage than you realize. If you've been making your payments on time (even if only the minimum amounts due), that credit-card company doesn't want to lose your business. So if you call and say that you have a better offer (or that you could get one) from another financial institution, they will probably lower your interest rate on the spot – or at least put your account under consideration for a rate reduction if you pay on time for, say, six months straight. They know it's a competitive market, and consumers get deluged with low-rate credit card and balance transfer options week after week. It's well worth it for a credit grantor to consider lowering your interest rate, than to lose your business altogether because you initiate a balance transfer from another company.

Six Things To Ask For

Here are the main objectives when you call a creditor about your account. Depending on your circumstances, you want the person on the other end of the phone to do any or all of the following:

- Lower your interest rate
- Stop late fees
- Eliminate over-the-limit charges
- Upgrade your account to "current" status
- Remove a negative mark from your credit
- Accept a partial payment in lieu of the total due

Before you contact credit card companies, however, there is something I'd like to share with you to help you separate the myths from the facts when you get ready to negotiate.

The Biggest Myth About Credit Card Cos.

I think the biggest myth about credit card companies is that they are big, impersonal institutions that aren't willing to budge to help consumers in financial trouble.

The reality is that credit card companies are run by individuals, and armed with the proper knowledge, perspective and strategy, you can get a lot of help from the right individual at these institutions.

Getting Your Creditors To Work With You

Probably the most productive thing you can do to get your creditors to work with you is to *initiate the process*. As painful as it might seem, yes, I want you to actually pick up the phone and *call them* – instead of the other way around. I know some of you have gotten used to ducking telephone calls from banks and department stores, asking your kids or family members to fib and say you aren't home, or disguising your voice to avoid dealing with your creditors. But beginning today, you're going to be proactive about knocking out your debts. And it starts with you figuring out a workable plan – something that works for the creditor, but something that you can also live with.

Be frank about your situation. If you have recently lost your job, are going through a divorce, have gotten sick and been unable to work, or whatever, let your creditors know about it. Again, part of your strategy (yes, it's strategy, but you only want to say what is honest and accurate) is to appeal to that person's sense of fairness and compassion. After all, you are dealing with another human being – even though some people who've been browbeaten by debt collectors might argue otherwise.

Now, I realize that it's not always realistic or practical to rely on someone else's willingness to help you out of a bind. In fact,

I've heard horror stories about consumers who tried to work out financial arrangements, only to be berated by debt collectors that used foul language and clearly had no compassion whatsoever. I'm not talking right now about dealing with collection agencies – they're a different story. I'm referring to your direct negotiations with creditors, like Visa, MasterCard, or Sears.

What's The Impact of a 16.9% Interest Rate?

Assume you want your credit card company to lower your interest rate – maybe from 16.9% to 5.9%.

To figure the simple annual interest on any debt, take the total amount you owe and multiply it times the interest rate expressed as a decimal. HINT: To get the rate shown as a decimal, just move the decimal over two places to the left.

So let's say you have a $3,000 Visa bill at 16.9% interest. Making minimum payments on a credit card with a $3,000 balance will take 16 years and 7 months to pay off. Why? You'll pay $60 a month, assuming your bank requires the typical minimum of 2% of your outstanding balance.

Annual Interest: $507

Let me show you how I got the annual interest of $507.

Note: the formula for figuring simple annual interest is:

Amount owed ($3,000) x Interest rate (shown as a decimal) (.169)

REMEMBER: to show the 16.9% interest rate as a decimal, I just moved the decimal over two places to the left.

So $3,000 x .169 = $507

Annual Interest = $507

But What If You Had A 5.9% Interest Rate?

You'd pay a lot less in finance charges and ...

You could knock out this debt in just one year.

Here's how:

New Annual Interest: $177

Your original debt of $3,000 plus $177 in annual interest totals $3,177. To get rid of that $3,177 in a year, you'd need to pay $264.75 a month, since:

$\underline{\$3,177 \text{ (total debt)}}$ = $264.75 (required monthly payment)

    12 (months)

In this example, negotiating to get a better interest rate would give you the ability to pay off this debt in one year instead of 16 years; and the lower 5.9% rate would also save you thousands of dollars in interest charges over time.

By the way, which way do you want interest to flow in your life? Realize that as a consumer, all you do is pay interest. Once you get financially fit and start saving and investing, you start to collect interest. Once you truly get the concept of interest, you'll probably agree with this statement:

*Those who understand interest are destined to **collect** it; those who don't are doomed to **pay** it for life.*

That statement is really just a variation of what the Bible teaches. Proverbs 22:7 says: "Just as the rich rule the poor, *so the borrower is servant to the lender*" (my emphasis added). So when you borrow, you become a slave, of sorts, to your creditor.

What's The Best Time To Negotiate With Creditors?

In most cases, it's best to deal with creditors *before* you actually miss a payment. Creditors are much more willing to work with you if you've paid your bills on time. They're trusting that you'll continue to honor your obligations – even if it means paying only minimum payments or even less than the minimums if that's an agreement that you stick with.

If your credit is already shot, at other times, it's often more advantageous to negotiate with creditors after the debt you owe is so old that the creditor has practically forgotten about it.

What do I mean by this? Let's look at the two following scenarios.

Say you lose your job unexpectedly. Statistics show that it's not easy – or fast – to find a replacement job. On average, it will take about one month to replace every $10,000 in income lost. So if you were among the top 1% of wage-earners in this country, and you had a six-figure job paying $100,000, it will probably take you about 10 months to find a similar-paying job. Likewise, if you were earning $40,000 a year, on average, it will take you four months time to find a comparable-paying position. In the meantime, if you don't think you can pay all your bills, start calling your creditors immediately. Ask them to lower your interest rate, even if only temporarily. Again, credit card companies and other lenders are much more willing to be flexible for people who take the time to initiate the process of working out a payment plan, a reduced interest deal, or whatever.

But let's say you have an old debt – a $2,000 bill that you racked up three years ago from a department store. For whatever reason, you never paid that bill and the store has already reported your non-payment on your credit report. The department store has also "written off" your account as a "bad debt expense." So if you come along now and offer to make a lump sum payment as a settlement in lieu of payment in full, chances are the creditor will go for it. After all, that company would probably rather get some money from you, than no money at all. If you work out one of these deals, however, make sure you get the creditor to first agree in writing that it will *completely delete* the negative history from your credit report if you send in the agreed-upon payment.

If a creditor just marks your past due account as "Paid" or "Paid as Agreed," that may do absolutely nothing for your credit score. They have to also agree to delete any references to late payments that they may have previously put on your credit report. Never let them "upgrade" your account status to "Paid Collection" or "Paid Charge-Off." Negative information can legally stay in your credit file for seven years, based on the date of "last activity." So changing your account to "Paid Charge-Off" restarts the clock, adding another 7-year negative mark to your file. Look at Appendix B for a Sample Settlement Letter to creditors to get them to agree to a settlement and remove negative marks from your credit file.

13 Negotiating Strategies To Lower Your Interest Rate, or Eliminate Late Fees and Over-The-Limit Charges

- Call in the morning

Don't call at the end of the day when customer service representatives are tired, more stressed and have been dealing all day with irate cardholders. Also avoid calling on the weekends; there may not be a supervisor there if you need one.

- Be polite in making any requests

Get the conversation off to a good start by using good manners. Say "hello" or "good morning" to the person you're talking to and call her by name, as in "Good morning, Susan, this is Kim Jones, I'm calling about my account." Make sure your tone sounds like you are making requests, not demands. Be friendly and conversational, not adversarial, to establish a good rapport and get the cooperation of the person on the other end of telephone.

- Request to speak to a supervisor if necessary

If you get nowhere with the person you're talking to, don't be afraid to "escalate" your phone call by asking to speak with a supervisor. Even if the conversation isn't confrontational or negative, you may require a manager because some employees will say they don't have the power to honor your request.

- Point out your length of time as a customer

For those of you who've been with a credit card company for a number of years, use your long-term status as leverage in asking for what you want.

- Emphasize how much business you've done

Many of you might have racked up a lot of charges over time. If you've been a valued customer by virtue of having charged many goods and services, make that known. And state that you also value the relationship with your creditor and would like to remain a customer in good standing.

- Stress your willingness pay what you owe

Creditors may not be inclined to be flexible with individuals they perceive as trying to "get over." The worst thing you can do is to convey the impression that you're a "deadbeat" who's out to weasel out of paying your obligations. A better strategy: stress that you are, in fact, willing and desirous of paying your bills.

- Reveal any extenuating circumstances

In cases where there have been out of the ordinary circumstances, let your creditors know this. For instance, if you lost your job, suffered a death in the family or something major happened in your life that caused you to miss a payment, tell them. Also make it clear if something happened that prevented you from getting your bills, such as you moved addresses or got divorced and your ex-got the statements. Creditors may be willing to waive late fees in such cases.

- Directly refer to your credit report

Don't be ashamed to say that a negative mark from the creditor could hurt your credit report – especially if you're in the market for a new car or house. Tell them your situation, and say something like, "I'd hate for this one blemish from your company to damage my credit standing or my ability to get a loan." Tip: only do this with your original creditors, who will likely be more sensitive to your predicament. Don't try this tactic with collection agents. That's giving them too much information, and they'll just use that information against you, saying, in effect: "If you don't pay up, you won't get that new house."

- Make "first-time" cases work in your favor

If you've never been late before or you've never had an over-the limit fee assessed, ask directly for a removal of a late fee or over-the-limit charge. A little-known fact is that many credit card companies give their employees the option (without even getting a supervisor's approval) of waiving late fees once every 12 months. If this is the case for you, do ask to get those fees removed. You might be surprised at how easily they will agree.

- Mention their competition

As a last resort, when you're negotiating for a lower interest rate, mention that you might be inclined to take your business elsewhere. The point here is not to make an idle threat. And I wouldn't start the conversation off with talk about you possibly going to a competitor. But you'd certainly be justified in exploring your options – and telling the creditor about other companies' balance transfer deals or lower interest-rate offers – if they won't budge on high interest rate cards.

- Document all conversations in writing

In the event you have to go back and get something corrected, or removed, it helps your case if you can refer to your written notes and say, "I spoke to XYZ person on this date, and was told such and such."

- Initiate requests immediately

Anytime you see there's an issue you want resolved, contact your creditor immediately. Don't wait a couple weeks, or even worse, a few months to ask for a rate reduction or removal of late fees. That works against you because it seems like you didn't care enough about the situation to do take instant action. It also reflects well on you when you initiate the call regarding late payments, as opposed to them having to contact you.

- Explain online payment discrepancies

If you were paying a bill online and for some reason payment didn't go through, that could be a legitimate reason for late fees to get removed. Another possibility: say you were making minimum payments on a credit card that had a teaser rate of 0% interest for six months. And assume you were paying $100 a month on that card via automatic online payments. Six months later, your teaser rate expired and the normal 14.9% rate kicked in. All of a sudden, your new minimum payment might be $115 a month. If you weren't keeping up with things, you would still be automatically sending in $100 payments online. The first time that happened, you'd likely get dinged with a late payment, for being $15 short in your payment. If you call the credit card company and point this out to them, they'll see your online payment history and will likely waive the late fee.

These techniques work. How do I know? I've used some of them, or have talked to many others, like Greg Lackowitz, who have successfully used these strategies. Lackowitz works at a television station in New York. He once called Discover and was able to get the interest on his credit card reduced from 18.9% to 7.9%.

Day 6 Switch cards if necessary.

If you have any creditors that won't budge on cards with sky-high interest rates (perhaps because you've missed a payment or two), be willing to switch the balance to a new card, if you can. To find good rates, call local banks, visit www.cardweb.com or log onto www.bankrate.com.

The Benefit of Comparison Shopping

I love both of these sites because they really empower consumers who are willing to comparison shop. And shopping around can really save you money and help you get a tailored credit card that addresses your circumstances. For example, at CardWeb.com, the company breaks credit cards down into 10 categories, allowing you to search for cards that fit your particular needs. The 10 categories are:

- Low rate (ranked by APR)
- Low Intro/Promotional Rate
- No Annual-Fee
- Premium (gold, platinum, etc.)
- Reward (gas, travel, cash-back, etc.)
- Secured (deposit required)
- Business
- Student
- Pre-paid/Gift Cards
- Smart Cards

You can apply online, and CardWeb.com tells you key information about each card, such as what the APR is, whether or not an annual fee is imposed, and how many days grace period you'll get.

Meanwhile, Bankrate.com gets a big thumbs up for its simplicity and user-friendly format for credit shoppers, as well as for the web site's vast assortment of helpful personal finance information.

At Bankrate.com, you can do things like check interest rates in your particular state, pose questions to the site's Debt Adviser, or bone up on the latest tactics for handling your credit by reading Bankrate's special sections on "Debt Consolidation," "Credit Scoring," and "Problem Credit."

Warnings About Obtaining New Credit

One caveat though: I don't recommend going out and opening up a slew of new credit card accounts – even if you get multiple teaser offers with initial low interest rates. Opening up too many accounts at once can actually hurt your credit score for two reasons. For starters, remember that length of credit history is one factor (approximately 15%) in determining your FICO® score. Generally speaking, the longer you have been managing credit, the more positive that influences your score. So if you open several new accounts, the average age of your accounts will decrease, possibly lowering your score.

Additionally, you don't want to have too many inquiries on your credit report. While you're shopping around for a better rate, try to do it all within a 14-day period. Fair Isaac says that it counts multiple inquiries made around the same time frame – say, for a new credit card or a new auto loan – as one single inquiry, so as not to penalize consumers who are comparison shopping. Also, your FICO® score ignores all inquires made in the 30 days before scoring, just to ensure that your score won't be lowered by this as a result of you hunting for the best deals.

Having said all this, credit inquiries still stay on your credit report for two years. And although credit inquiries don't impact your score all that much, one additional inquiry can take up to five points off your FICO® score, according to Fair Isaac.

Another insider tip: Don't believe it when people say that getting rid of your credit cards will improve your credit. "Closing your credit card accounts almost never helps your score and most likely will hurt it," says Fair Isaac's Ryan Sjoblad.

Here's the bottom line: Don't open a barrage of new credit card accounts. But having one new account with a single digit interest rate – or perhaps a 0% offer for six months – can save you big bucks. Also, don't just close out or cancel all your old credit card accounts; again, that might reduce your credit score.

Day 7 Always exceed the minimum payment due.

Creditors typically ask that you pay about 2% of your outstanding balance. That's a great way for them to get rich – but you'll be a customer for life, taking many years to pay off goods and services you charged ages ago. If you can swing it, I recommend always paying at least three times the required minimum amount due.

"Minimum" Payments Now Really Equal Maximum Payments In the Long-Run

Paying so-called minimum payments now really ends up costing you more – a lot more – in the long run. The math behind some of the calculations that determine your interest rate can be tricky. And I won't get into all the complex, and sometimes mind-boggling formulas that are used to calculate your Annual Percentage Rate (APR). But suffice to say that for every $1,000 you owe, if you paid the normal minimum of just 2%, you'd only be paying $20 a month. With just $2,500 in debt on a card with an 18.5% interest rate, you'd spend 30 years paying it off.

A Guaranteed Investment Return

Many charge cards carry very high interest rates of 18% to 21% or more. If you carry large credit card balances, that's a drain on your monthly finances. At the very least, start doubling up on your payments in order to pay off those credit cards sooner, rather than later. If you pay off a MasterCard that is charging you 21% interest, that's the equivalent to earning a guaranteed 21% investment return – and you won't find that kind of guarantee anywhere in the stock market.

But I Don't Have the Money!

I know some of you may be saying: "I don't have the money! If I had the money to pay three times my minimum balance – or even all of it, I would've done it by now!" Well, keep reading – particularly in **Days 15** through **24** – for ideas about how you're going to come up with the money to ultimately achieve Zero Debt status. For now, to get you on track, I want you to write a check this day to *pay more than the minimum due* on one credit card that you owe. I don't care if it's a $5 check. Just pay extra money on any *one* bill right now. It can be on a card you've already paid this month or an upcoming bill. But mail that check *today*!

Week Number 2

This week you will:

- Dispute any inaccuracies in your credit file
- Educate yourself about your legal rights
- Halt creditor harassment
- Guard against identity theft to shield your credit
- Set up a good filing and record-keeping system
- Face the truth about your financial situation
- Create SMART financial goals

Day 8 Dispute any inaccuracies in your credit file.

Under a federal law called the Fair Credit Reporting Act, you have the right to have erroneous information deleted from your credit report. So if anything is wrong in your credit file, just write the credit bureaus at the addresses found at the end of this book, and state your dispute. Errors include closed accounts that are still shown as open, data about accounts you did not open, or negative items, such as bankruptcies or liens, from someone else with a similar name or social security number. The credit bureaus have 30 days to investigate your claims. After that, they must remove any information that is found to be inaccurate or that can no longer be verified.

How Accurate Are Credit Reports?

According to a number of consumers groups in the United States, many credit reports are filled with inaccuracies. The Consumer Federation of America (CFA) and the National Credit Reporting Association (NCRA) once released a landmark study that found that millions of Americans were in jeopardy of being denied credit or unnecessarily paying more for loans because of mistakes in their credit files.

The CFA and the NCRA analyzed the credit scores of some 500,000 consumers nationwide. Then they examined dozens of credit files in great detail. Their conclusions were alarming:

- Errors of omission and commission were fairly common (Some 200 million Americans have credit files, and the CFA and NCRA believe that millions of those credit files – perhaps as many as 70% – may contain mistakes)
- 78% of credit files were missing an account that was in good standing (possibly hurting people's FICO® scores)
- 33% of files were missing a mortgage account that had never been late (more positive, but absent data)
- If errors in a person's credit report caused her to pay "sub-prime" rates for a mortgage, those mistakes could cost the consumer dearly. Having a credit score below a cut off mark – namely a FICO® score of 620 points – meant an individual would pay roughly $124,000 more for a $150,000 fixed-rate, 30-year mortgage
- 43% of files had conflicting information from Equifax, Experian and TransUnion concerning how many times a customer was 30 days late on a payment

How Do Mistakes In Your Credit File Occur?

Many errors in your credit report revolve around the fact that the information listed about you is not complete, it is not updated, or it actually describes someone else. Mistakes in your credit file can happen in any number of ways, but most of them are the result of human error. For instance, you might accidentally give someone the wrong social security number. Or maybe an administrative assistant or salesman read your social security number incorrectly on an application or they typed it in wrong on a computer.

In other cases, errors in your credit file can occur if you apply for credit under different names (i.e. William Johnson, Bill Johnson, etc.) Sometimes family members get their credit histories crisscrossed, as when a Joe Jones Senior finds that his credit file erroneously contains some of Joe Jones Junior's credit information. "It's amazing how many times Juniors and Seniors get mixed up," says Fair Isaac's Sjoblad, who also used to work for a credit-reporting company, and saw credit file errors first-hand.

Credit Errors Can Cost You Money And More

No matter how the mistake occurs, errors in your credit report can cost you money, as illustrated above by the study conducted by the Consumer Federation of America and the National Credit Reporting Association. With incorrect information in your credit file, you also run the risk of being denied basic services – like utilities or cell phone service – as well as more crucial things, like getting insurance or a new job.

Fixing Errors & Cleaning Up Your Credit File

Some errors can be dealt with immediately. Others require a serious letter-writing campaign. Start out by going directly to your creditor and requesting that they delete outdated or negative information that is inaccurate from your credit report.

Consumers sometimes mistakenly write to the credit bureaus asking them, in effect to change their credit report. But agencies like Equifax, Experian and TransUnion only gather information that is sent to them from your creditors. They in turn report that information. The only time they will "change" something on your credit is if you put in a formal, written request disputing something in your credit file. As noted earlier, the credit bureaus have 30 days to investigate your claims.

After you've received your credit report, if it's something as simple as old information that needs to be deleted, just write the credit bureau a letter to that effect. Do the same thing if you notice that there are multiple accounts being reported for what is essentially the same bill due (this happened to me once when I had a ton of student loans and consolidated them with Sallie Mae). You don't want it to seem like you have more credit/bills outstanding than you actually do.

If the mistake pertains to an account that is not yours, again, write the bureaus and tell them this. They will usually take it off without a problem if the account can't be verified.

Sometimes, however, you ask your creditor to delete negative information that you believe is incorrect, or you write the credit bureaus and still get nowhere. What then? Don't despair. You still have the option of including a 100-word statement in your credit file, stating your side of things. For instance, if a debt in dispute was not your account because it was opened solely by your former husband (or ex-wife), explain in your statement that the account was your ex-spouse's and now you're divorced.

Raising Your FICO® Score

Getting rid of mistakes in your credit file can raise your FICO® score, because your score is based on the information contained in your credit report(s). Some simple strategies to raise your FICO® score include:

- Pay your bills on time and keep them up to date
- Keep your balances as low as humanly possible on credit cards and other "revolving" credit accounts
- Pay down your debt, rather than moving it around
- Refrain from opening a rash of accounts all at once
- Secure new credit selectively, and over time, to re-establish credit if you've had difficulties in the past

Improve Your Credit Score in 3 Days – Legally

If you're applying for a mortgage, and you think an error on your credit report will get you turned down or cause you to pay a higher interest rate, you *must* read my advice in **Day 23**. I'll reveal a legitimate way you can quickly raise your credit score. It's called "Credit Re-Scoring" and it's a legal, fast way to fix errors in your credit file and improve your credit standing – in most cases in as little as two or three days. The National Association of Mortgage Brokers started this rapid dispute process in 1998, after its members saw how many errors in credit reports were preventing borrowers from getting loans or forcing them to paying unfairly high interest rates. Again, to learn about credit re-scoring, see the suggestions I make about managing mortgage debt in **Day 23** of *Zero Debt*.

Day 9 Educate yourself about your legal rights.

As a consumer, you have a multitude of rights under the law as it pertains to your debt. Perhaps the strongest measure of all is the Fair Debt Collection Practices Act, also known as Public Law 95-109. Passed in 1977, this law protects consumers from harassment, abuse or unfair actions by collection agencies.

When your account goes so far past due that your creditor doesn't think it's likely that you'll pay up, that creditor will often write your debt off as un-collectable. To get some money, however, the creditor can sell your debt to a third party collection agency, or hire that collection agency to work on a commission basis to try to recover some of the money you owe.

By the time a debt collector enters the picture, as you may know, your credit has already taken a hit. But here's where it can get really nasty. Debt collection firms have been known to use every tactic under the sun – including legal and illegal means – to force consumers to pay their bills. If a collection agency comes after you, you may be subjected to any or all of the following things:

- coercion
- threats
- lies/deception
- intimidation
- fear
- blackmail
- harassment
- constant phone calls

It may or may not surprise you to learn that all of these tactics are ILLEGAL. For example, creditors can't claim that you will be arrested, curse at or verbally threaten you, or call you at all hours (such as before 8 a.m. and after 9 p.m. your local time) – even though such ploys are common, according to John Bowe, a collection agent from Hempstead, New York.

"If the debt collector realizes that they debtor is ignorant of the law, he'll try to skirt the law," says Bowe, who's seen it all.

10 Rights Protecting Consumers

There are 10 major areas within the Fair Debt Collections Practice Act that are designed to safeguard your rights. Read this chapter carefully. It will arm you with virtually everything you need to know to end to any illegal debt collection practices you might be enduring. The bottom line is that just because you owe money, that doesn't give debt collection firms the right to treat you unfairly. Here are the 10 safeguards for consumers:

1. **How Creditors Track You Down**

   This area of the law is formally called "Acquisition of Location Information." It basically limits what debt-collectors can do to legally find you. For instance, debt collectors:

   - Can't tell third parties, such as your boss or neighbors that they're trying to reach you about a debt
   - Shall only say to others that they're trying to confirm or correct your location (and not mention your debt)

- Must not communicate with any one else (like your supervisor) more than once, unless the debt collector believes the location information given was erroneous or incomplete
- Are not supposed to mail you anything via postcard, either at home or at your place of employment
- Can't use any kind of mailing, envelope, or other communication that would let someone else know that the company is a debt collection agency
- Are prohibited from contacting you once you notify them in writing that you are represented by an attorney and give them the attorney's name/address

2. The Way Debt Collectors Communicate About You

This area of the law prevents collection agencies from hounding you or trying to embarrass you by telling others your personal business. The law states that debt collectors:

- Can't communicate with you before 8 am. Or after 9 p.m. (your local time) unless you give them permission or they have a court order to do so
- Can't contact you if you've notified them that a lawyer is representing you
- Can't call you on the job if you tell them that your employer prohibits you from receiving such calls
- Can't talk about your situation with anyone; not your friends, relatives, neighbors or co-workers. The only ones

they can discuss your debts with are your attorney, the original creditor and credit-reporting agencies.

3. Prohibitions Against Harassment or Abuse

No debt collector is legally allowed to harass, abuse or oppress you – under any circumstances whatsoever. Any of the following tactics are violations of the Fair Debt Collection Practices Act:

- The use of violence, or the threat of it, or any criminal action that would hurt a person's body, property or reputation
- Obscene or profane language (verbal or written)
- Publishing any lists (except to a credit bureau) that shows consumers who refused to pay a debt
- Threatening or actually posting the debt for sale to another party in order to compel repayment
- Constantly calling an individual on the telephone or engaging a consumer in repeated conversations with the intention to annoy, abuse or harass someone

4. False or Misleading Representations

Collection agencies are prohibited from making false or misleading representations to consumers in the course of trying to secure debt repayment. Some violations of the law in this area include:

- Falsely stating or implying that the debt collector is bonded by, or associated with any federal or state government entity

- Falsely representing the nature of any debt, the amount owed, the legal status of the account, or compensation paid to the collection agency for recovering the debt

- Falsely claiming that the debt collector is an attorney or represents an attorney

- Falsely asserting that you will be imprisoned or arrested if you don't pay your bills (debtors' prisons don't exist anymore in this country)

- Falsely representing that your failure to pay could result in your wages being garnished, your property being seized, or your assets being sold – unless such measures are lawful, and unless the debt collector actually intends to take those actions

- Falsely stating such misinformation such as the documents they send to you represent a legal process or that the debt collector works for a credit bureau

5. Unfair Practices

No debt collector can use dishonest or unfair means of making you pay your debts. The following actions are deemed to be violations of the law:

- Collecting any money at all – such as interest, late fees or charges other than the principal amount – unless it is specifically permitted by law and/or authorized by the agreement that created the debt

- Taking post-dated checks from you that are more than five days away, unless the debt collector informs you no more than 10 or less than three business days before depositing the check
- Soliciting postdated checks for the purpose of threatening or instituting criminal prosecution
- Depositing or threatening to deposit any postdated check before the date of such check
- Making collect calls to consumers, or doing anything that would cause debtors to incur charges for communication by debt collectors that are trying to conceal the purpose of their contact

6. Validation of Debts

As a consumer, you have the right to verify, validate or dispute any debt you are told about, within a given time frame. Within five days of initially contacting you, a debt collection agency must:

- Send you a written notice containing the amount of the debt, the name of the credit, a statement informing you of your right to dispute it within 30 days, and a statement indicating that if you contest any portion of the debt, the debt collector will obtain verification of the debt and mail it to you

- Supply you with the name and address of the original creditor if different from the current creditor (if you ask for this info in writing)
- Cease collection attempts during the "verification of debt" period, if you dispute the debt or ask for the name and address of the original creditor

7. Multiple Debts

The law protects your repayment rights when you owe multiple debts to creditors. In this case, debt collectors:

- May not apply any payments you make to any debt that you dispute
- Must follow your instructions about how you want debts repaid (i.e. which debt should be paid first on your outstanding balances)

8. Legal Action By Debt Collectors

Federal law limits where debt collectors can bring legal proceedings against consumers that owe money. In general, any debt collector initiating legal action shall:

- Bring legal action against real property only in a judicial district or similar legal entity where the property is located
- Barring the above provision, debt collectors can bring action in judicial district where the consumer signed the contract or where he/she currently lives

9. Furnishing Certain Deceptive Forms

Debt collection agencies are prohibited from supplying you with misleading or deceptive forms in a bid to make you pay your debts. The Fair Debt Collections Reporting Act states that it is unlawful for:

- Debt collectors to design compile or furnish any form knowing that such a form would create a false belief or a false impression that anyone other than the debt collection agency is participating in the collection activity (for example, debt collectors can't falsely claim lawyers or government agencies are involved)

10. Civil Liability

When debt collectors break the law, they can be sued for failing to abide by federal rules and forced to pay:

- The actual damages sustained
- Additional damages up to $1,000 (for an individual)
- The lesser of $500,000 or 1% of the debt collector's net worth (in the case of a class action lawsuit)

If you believe a debt collection firm has violated any of these laws in dealing with you, report the company at once to your state Attorney General's office and the Federal Trade Commission at www.ftc.gov or 877-FTC-HELP.

And make no mistake, in addition to breaches of the Fair Debt Collections Practices Act, violations of the Fair Credit Reporting Act also happen. For instance, Pennsylvania-based NCO Group, which is one of America's biggest debt collection firms, agreed in May 2004 to pay regulators a record $1.5 million to settle charges brought by the Federal Trade Commission that NCO Group routinely violated the FCRA by reporting inaccurate information about consumer accounts to credit-reporting agencies. That $1.5 million settlement was the largest-ever civil penalty ever obtained in a FCRA case. The settlement also requires NCO to implement a monitoring program to review all complaints received and make sure that reporting errors are corrected quickly.

As a consumer, you have to stand up for yourself when dealing with debt collectors. Yes, you may owe money, but that doesn't give them the right to harass or treat you unfairly.

One final tip: if you agree to payment arrangements, never send postdated checks to a collection agency. Instead, send in money orders, suggests Bowe, the collection agent. He says collection agencies have been known to deposit checks earlier than agreed, or to "accidentally or intentionally" debit your checking account for an amount higher than what was agreed. Either way, if there's a mix-up, "now you have to fight to get your money back, and that might be a slow process," says Bowe.

Day 10 Stop collection agency harassment.

If any debt collection firms are harassing you – and you now know from the previous chapter that harassment is illegal – you can make them stop immediately.

"Cease Contact" or "Cease and Desist" Letter

Simply write a two-sentence letter advising them to cease all contact with you. The first sentence should say: "I am unable to pay this bill because …" or "I refuse to pay this debt because…" and explain your reason. You also have the option of not providing a reason at all. The second sentence should state: "I hereby assert my right, under Section 805-C of the Fair Debt Collection Practices Act, to request that you cease any further communication with me."

After they receive your "Cease & Desist" letter, debt collection firms can't contact you, except to indicate that the collection process against you has stopped, or that they plan to take, or recommend that your original creditor take, legal action against you, such as taking you to court. Even then, debt collectors can't threaten legal action unless they *truly* intend to take it. Either way, the annoying phone calls and those harassing letters will immediately end.

"Usually (collectors) will say they'll proceed with court action and it's not true," says collection agent John Bowe. "They'll say things like 'Your wages will be garnished' even if it's not true, because collectors will walk right over a person who's ignorant of the law. Knowing the Fair Debt Collections Practices Act is the debtors best tool against collection agents."

Using the U.S. Post Office

When you send your "Cease & Desist" letter, make absolutely sure that you send it Certified Mail, Return Receipt Requested. I can't stress enough the importance of taking this step. "You definitely want to send the letter certified mail," cautions Bowe. "If it's not send certified, they'll probably say it got lost in the mail and contact you again."

Your Certified Mail receipt from the Post office will be your proof of mailing. And having that Return Receipt – signed by an employee at the collection agency – will bolster your claims if you get embroiled in a legal dispute.

I don't care how broke you are; don't send off any Cease & Desist Letters if they're not processed through the U.S. Postal Service as Certified Mail-Return Receipt Requested. Otherwise, you'll be sorry. And you'll have wasted your time. To send a letter Certified Mail will cost you $2.30, in addition to your postage charges. To get your proof of delivery, fill out Form 3811 (the Return Receipt form) at the Post Office. That will cost you another $1.75. Again, don't fret over these charges; it's money well spent.

In Appendix C of *Zero Debt*, you will find a sample Cease & Desist Letter. This basic language is all you need to say to debt collectors to get them off your back.

Day 11 Prevent identity theft to protect your credit.

There are at least seven million cases of identity theft annually. Identity theft occurs when someone steals your private information, such as your driver's license or social security number, and uses that data for his or her own personal gain, to open credit accounts or take out loans in your name.

Tips To Avoid Identity Theft

To protect yourself from identity theft, don't carry your social security card with you, leave most credit cards at home, and shred sensitive mail (don't just trash it). There was a time when crooks misappropriated consumers' identities by rifling through their trash, stealing their mail, or by looking over their shoulders at ATM machines, etc. Nowadays, an identity thief is just a likely to pull a high-tech con on you, convincing you to give up your information over the Internet, or stealing your data by hacking into corporate databases.

Sadly, a growing number of identity theft victims have this dreadful white-collar crime perpetrated against them by their own family members or loved ones. Cases abound of siblings opening accounts in their sisters' or brothers' names; there are adult children making unauthorized charges on their parents credit cards; and some parents are even doing their own minor children a disservice by getting credit in the name and/or social security number of the child. They probably don't realize that their credit binge right now could ruin that child's credit for many, many years to come.

Identity Theft In The Workplace

But what most people don't know is that the fastest growing place where identity theft occurs is in the workplace.

Employees nationwide face all kinds of worries on the job: everything from meeting tight deadlines to the threat of downsizing. Now experts say there's another challenge confronting U.S. workers: Identity theft in the workplace is on the rise.

"You can not under-estimate how important the workplace is in protecting your personal financial information," says Carl Pergola, the New York-based director of BDO Seidman's national fraud investigation practice.

According to credit reporting agency TransUnion, theft from employers' records or other businesses that collect data on consumers is now the top source of identity fraud.

In some cases, disgruntled employees hack into computer databases to steal private information. But in most instances, personnel information is more readily obtained simply because this data is not carefully guarded. Additionally, large numbers of people at work may have access to information such as your date of birth, social security or driver's license numbers.

Pergola calls identity theft a crime of opportunity, one that can be committed by "co-workers, receptionists ... anyone who can get access to your information."

The Identity Theft Resource Center in San Diego estimates that there are between seven million and 10 million cases of identity theft annually.

"The average victim is going to spend around 175 to 200 hours of their time cleaning up the mess left by an identity thief," says Jay Foley, the Center's director of victim's services. Victims also typically lose about $1,000 due to time away from work, and out-of-pocket expenses, he adds.

"The problem is that too much personal information is collected at the job," says Linda Foley, executive director of the Identity Theft Resource Center. She highlights several areas of concern:

- Job applications that require social security numbers
- Timecards that mandate social security information and are stored in public areas
- Health insurance cards with social security numbers as the membership numbers
- Unlocked personnel file cabinets
- The absence of locking drawers in many cubicles

Compounding the problem, employees are often reluctant to report identity theft to their bosses. "Employers sometimes have an unwritten policy: 'Don't bring your personal problems to work.' So victims may not want to draw attention to themselves," says Linda Foley.

Scams Affect Workers And Those Looking For Work

Widespread layoffs across corporate America are also giving rise to another work-related identity theft con known as "the resume scam." In this swindle, con artists post fake job listings in newspapers or on the Internet. When you respond with a resume, they call or e-mail you and request more background information. But once they get your personal data, they disappear. Much later, you discover unauthorized credit purchases or newly opened accounts in your name.

Linda Foley says educating people about ways to protect themselves against this kind of deception is often "a double-edged sword."

"The minute we go public about a scam, while it helps to tell consumers what to avoid, it also gives ideas to criminals about what to do," she says.

Here are some ways to limit your chances of falling victim to identity theft on the job:

- Don't carry your social security card in your wallet
- Leave credit cards at home unless absolutely necessary
- Ask your employer to keep personnel information in a secure environment
- Request a locking drawer or storage area for your personal items – and use it constantly. (Explain to your boss that you don't want to carry your purse, bag or briefcase with you

each time you leave your desk to get coffee, go to the restroom, or attend a meeting)

Despite your own personal efforts, realize that it will take a change in business practices to stem the tide of workplace identity theft. Says Linda Foley: "The first line of defense in combating this problem always has been – and always will be – the business community. Because that's where the majority of information is collected, stored, and maintained."

Identity Theft Insurance

Fair Isaac Corporation, parent of myFICO, offers an identity theft insurance product for sale. If you check out www.myfico.com, you'll see that the cost of the insurance for the standard product runs between $1.95 and $3.95 per month. For the deluxe product, consumers pay between $4.95 and $7.95 a month. Each one gives you weekly monitoring from over 400 data sources, email alerts when your personal information changes, and a $25,000 identity theft insurance policy.

The Insurance Information Institute (III) also reports that a handful of insurance companies have begun offering identity theft protection.

The insurance reimburses crime victims for the costs they incur in restoring their identity and repairing their credit reports – anything from lost wages to phone bills to sometimes attorneys fees. The policies are sold as either part of a homeowner's policy, or as a stand-alone policy or an endorsement to a homeowner's or renter's insurance policy. You can get an identity theft insurance policy from the following firms:

American International Group
www.aig.com

Chubb Group of Insurance Companies
www.chubb.com

Encompass Insurance
www.encompassinsurance.com

Farmers Group Inc.
www.farmers.com

Travelers Insurance
www.travelers.com

Years ago, I used to think that such insurance was unnecessary. But as identity theft has become such a widespread occurrence, I've changed my mind. If you can afford it, identity theft coverage is certainly worth a look.

It's gotten so bad that identity thieves are even stealing companies' identities. In 2004, a 39-year-old paralegal named Phoebe Nicholson was arrested and charged with grand larceny for allegedly embezzling $600,000 in a complex identity-theft scam. Authorities accused Nicholson of setting up a bank account in a name that was nearly identical to that of a New York law firm. The Manhattan law firm is Fish & Neave. Nicholson's bank account was set up under the name "Fish Neave." Nicholson allegedly then created seven bogus legal bills, and got her former employer, aerospace giant Honeywell, to pay the bills by forging her boss's signature. She then reportedly deposited the checks into the fraudulent bank account and later withdrew the money. "I guess if identity theft involving individuals is the fastest-growing crime, it was just a matter of time before we saw identity theft of corporations," Westchester County District Attorney Jeanine Pirro said in published reports.

Guess what Nicholson allegedly did with the cash? She paid off her mortgage, credit cards and other bills! Apparently, she too wanted Zero Debt. That doesn't excuse thievery. But this case does show how debt drives people to do desperate things.

What to Do if Your Identity is Stolen

Don't be shy about reaching out for help if your identity is stolen. Ignoring the problem won't make it go away. The sooner you act, the better. Report identity theft at once to the three major credit bureaus. They will put an "alert" on your credit file and you will be able to get a free copy of your credit report. Make a point to regularly check your credit file from now on. Sometimes identity thieves don't instantly go on shopping sprees – either because they're selling your information to others or because they're just laying low. In either case, you may not see any suspicious activity – like unauthorized charges or new accounts you didn't open – until months later. You should also immediately report identity theft to your local police department, and the Federal Trade Commission (www.ftc.gov or 877-ID-THEFT). For help and other resources, contact the Identity Theft Resource Center in San Diego at www.idtheftcenter.org or call 858-693-7935.

Day 12 Set up a good filing system.

One of the best things you can do to get financially fit in this year is to get yourself financially organized. So many of us want to whip our finances into shape, yet the task seems especially daunting because most households are overwhelmed by mounds of paperwork. But wouldn't it be great to have an easy, workable system for organizing all your financial documents – like those numerous credit card receipts, old bills, tax records, and quarterly investment statements? Well, here are some tips from a few experts that will help you get a handle on all your paperwork, streamline your home or office, better balance your time, and enhance your records and document management skills. As of today you're going to create an easy-to-use filing and financial record-keeping system.

Being Organized Helps Your Finances

In case you need any motivation, first consider all the benefits of getting rid of piles upon piles of paperwork and creating, for example, a decent filing system for your financial records. In the book "Let Go of Clutter," author Harriet Schechter says well-organized people can eliminate clutter and the stress related to it. They can also prevent piles of mail from accumulating, shed sentimental stuff without regret, and manage "mental clutter," she says.

Creating An Effective Filing System

To make an effective filing system, experts recommend alphabetizing your relevant documents by subject or category. But don't make the mistake of having too many or too few categories. A dozen broad categories should be the maximum in any filing system, Schechter says. Therefore, a sample file index might include categories for:

- Banking records (including checking and savings accounts)
- Bills paid (where you file regular monthly expenses)
- Budget (for itemized listings of all your expenses, income and assets)
- Credit cards (useful for storing receipts, statements and contracts)
- Insurance (auto, health, life and property insurance records)
- Investments (such as 401(k) and mutual fund reports)
- Mortgage
- Receipts
- Taxes

What To Keep – And What To Throw Away

Once you've gotten your files labeled, you may wonder how long you should keep certain financial documents. "As a rule, you should keep old tax records for at least seven years because that's how far back the law allows the IRS to go when it wants to audit you," says David Bach, a New York financial advisor and the author of *Smart Women Finish Rich*.

You should also hang on indefinitely to your stock, bond and mutual fund statements – mainly because if you sell any of those investments later, you may need to demonstrate the cost basis of your investment to the IRS. Bach notes, however, that you don't need to keep those prospectuses that mutual fund companies mail you each quarter, so you can safely toss those.

Additionally, Schechter says "when it doubt, throw it out," when it comes to things like magazine articles, seminar handouts and other "resource" materials you may have collected over the years.

Maintaining Your Filing System

Once you've got a working system, of course the final step is to stay on top of your paperwork, so that it doesn't spiral out of control again. Experts say you should resist the urge to have general mail files – like the dreaded, all-purpose "in" and "out" baskets that seem to occupy almost every home office and work desk space. Instead, create a paper-flow system that instantly tells you what you're supposed to do with the mail that's held there. For example, to quickly sort through mail – and it's best to do that the same day that it arrives – you can put it into categories labeled:

- "To Pay" (for bills, charitable solicitations, etc.)
- "To Read,"
- "To File,"
- "Correspondence,"

- "Pending/Follow-ups,"
- "Events/Invitations," or
- "To Share/Forward."

Once you weed through your files, purging unnecessary paperwork and reducing the amount of piles you have stacked up, chances are you'll be a lot clearer about your finances – and certainly better organized. What's more, if you take a few minutes each day to tackle your paperwork, you'll save yourself many hours – if not days – of having to wade through a morass of papers later in the year when you're trying to find some important document. This is particularly true when tax time rolls around. Imagine how great it would feel if you didn't have to go sifting through old piles of paper trying to justify all your tax deductions. Instead, you could simply turn over to your accountant or to a paid tax professional a nice, neat file of well-organized receipts and records. I can't guarantee you that you'll be paying Zero Taxes ... but I can promise you that having organized paperwork and a well-kept filing system is a strategy that will make tax time a lot less taxing!

Day 13 Face the truth about your situation.

Is your financial house in excellent, good, fair, poor or dire condition? Often, circumstances beyond our control or unexpected life events such as divorce, job loss or a death in the family can ruin one's finances. But in this chapter, I want you to consider also all the things *you* have done – both positive and negative – that have put your financial house in its present state.

Your Finances & The Laws of Cause and Effect

As a money coach, I teach a workshop called "Get Financially Fit Now!" One lesson that I tell participants is:

Your current financial situation is directly tied to your own actions (or lack thereof), because your finances operate according to the laws of "cause and effect."

What this means is that we have to first look in the mirror and determine what financial mistakes we have been making and what actions we might have taken to cause or continue our financial troubles. In some cases, it may not have been what we've done, but what we've procrastinated about, or failed to do, that has led to financial difficulties.

Again, there are certainly events that happen – such as illnesses or accidents – that are no fault of our own. But what I'm talking about are the financial problems we face that can be directly attributed to actions we have taken, or have neglected to take. Let's stop talking money for a minute and look beyond the economic world. Instead, let's examine other areas of life: the physical, natural and mechanical realms. Each area illustrates the laws of "cause and effect."

Physical Realm

When obesity occurs, frequently it is caused by improper nutrition and a lack of exercise. Barring some medical condition that causes one to gain weight, doctors agree that they best way to restore oneself to a proper weight and good health is to eat right and exercise regularly. If you fail to do this, obesity results.

Natural Realm

You don't need a green thumb to know that dying plants or a weed-filled garden are often caused by lack of water, insufficient sunlight, or inadequate pruning. To get that garden back in good condition, you must tend to it and give it proper care.

Mechanical Realm

The reason auto manufacturers suggest you change your car's oil every 3,000 miles is because a lack of maintenance or excessive wear and tear will cause your vehicle to break down. Just like you get regular checkups at the doctor, so too should your car get regular checkups at the mechanic.

In What Condition Is Your Financial House?

Whenever something is neglected or abused – no matter whether it's your body, your garden or your car – that thing will suffer. And the first order of business to get into good condition is to apply some care and attention.

The same principle holds true in the economic realm. When you neglect or abuse your financial house, the result is that it is in disrepair. And it won't get into tip-top condition until you start taking positive steps and stop doing the things that are detrimental to your financial condition.

So, here's your next action item: Make a list of what you have done right, and where you have clearly gone astray in conducting your personal financial affairs. Evaluate your past behavior as far as handling credit, paying bills on time, and managing your money. Whatever your present circumstances, I'd like for you to also think about how long your situation has been this way. Has it been less than a year, more than a year, two to five years, five to 10 years, or as long as you can remember?

Take 10 minutes or so and fill in the worksheet on the following page. It will guide you in your thinking and help you to face the truth about your current situation.

My Financial House

Instructions: Fill in the blanks with the correct statements.

My financial house is in _____ condition.
(excellent, good, fair, poor, or dire)

It has been that way for _____.
(Less than a year, more than a year, 2 to 5 years, 5 to 10 years, or as long as I can remember)

These are the things, good or bad, that I have done to put my financial house in its current state:
1. _____

2. _____

3. _____

4. _____

5. _____

These are the things I have neglected, or failed to do, that have resulted in my current financial condition:
1. _____

2. _____

3. _____

4. _____

5. _____

Your Financially Fit Check-up

Now I want you to take a quiz. It's a short, 10-question, true or false quiz. I call it the "Financially Fit Check-up."

I also give this quiz at seminars and workshops across the country – to investors who have a million dollars in net worth or better and to unemployed people who are having trouble putting food on the table.

Don't be scared by the prospect of taking this little test. This quiz is just a snapshot of where you are today. It's meant to see how "Financially Fit" you are by examining the extent to which you've handled some financial matters in your life.

It's not intended to be a comprehensive look at your finances, nor is it meant to predict where you'll be, say, a year from now. It's simply designed to help give you a look at how things are – right here and now.

After you take the quiz, view the "Financially Fit Score Guide" on the following page, then "grade" your quiz. Two requests: first, don't cheat yourself! Answer the questions honestly. Also, don't look ahead to the score guide just yet. Read it *after* you've actually taken the Financially Fit Quiz.

Financially Fit Check-up

Please read the following 10 statements. Answer "true" or "false" as appropriate for you.

		T	F
1.	I have enough money to buy, do or achieve the things I want.	___	___
2.	I know exactly how much debt I owe and how much it costs me each month/year in interest.	___	___
3.	I never worry about bills.	___	___
4.	I feel financially secure.	___	___
5.	I have a written financial plan.	___	___
6.	I have an updated will.	___	___
7.	I know that I have adequate life and disability insurance.	___	___
8.	I have an emergency cash cushion of at least 3 months' expenses.	___	___
9.	I have a very clear idea about where my money goes each month.	___	___
10.	I feel confident about my money-management knowledge/skills.	___	___

Lynnette Khalfani

Financially Fit Score Guide

DIRECTIONS: Give yourself 1 point for each "true" answer and 0 for
each "false" answer. Add and enter your score here: ————

8-10 Points: You have an extremely high degree of financial security and well-being.
You are very "Financially Fit."

5-7 Points: You are on the right path to becoming "Financially Fit." You have made
some wise choices and could benefit from making additional smart money moves.

2-4 Points: You are a good candidate to take some major steps to get "Financially Fit."

0-1 Point: Your financial health is in serious jeopardy. You need to immediately
develop a plan and take action to get out of the economic Intensive Care Unit and into the
"Financially Fit" Recovery Room.

Copyright Lynnette Khalfani www.themoneycoach.net

How Does Your Score Compare To Others?

You get 1 point for each "True" response and 0 points for each "False" response. The maximum score is 10 points. I've given this quiz to many thousands of people nationwide. And in case you are fretting over your score, let me tell you that roughly 70% of all the individuals who take this quiz score between 0 and 3.

I once gave a presentation at Rutgers University in Princeton, New Jersey where 2,000 people attended my seminar. In that crowd of 2,000, the highest score was a 7. Only one person – a 72-year-old retiree from Long Island named Maria – has ever scored a perfect 10. That says a lot about the state of most Americans' personal finances.

Needless to say, you don't have to score a perfect 10 in order to be "Financially Fit." But you should certainly aim for a score of at least 6 or 7. If you follow the advice contained throughout *Zero Debt*, you can definitely do that – at a minimum.

Now that you've examined your financial house, and reflected on what you may have done (or not done) to cause your current situation, I want you to write out three things you're going to quickly do to improve your finances.

Here's what I'm going to do about it …

In 24 hours, I will:_____

Within one week, I will:_____

Within one month, I will:_____

After you follow through on any one of your action items, write me at lynnette@themoneycoach.net to tell me about your progress.

Day 14 Create SMART financial goals.

SMART is an abbreviation for goals that are Specific, Measurable, Action-Oriented, Realistic, and Time-Bound. The idea is to avoid general, vague or hazy goals such "I want to be rich." Exactly what does *rich* mean to you? Is it having $100,000, or $1 million in the bank? And what's your timetable and/or deadline?

The Importance of Written Goals

You must have precise, written goals – *not ideas in your head.* If you can't come up with your own written goals and the plan that will get you there, find a local financial planner for help. You can contact one in your area through the Financial Planning Association at 800-647-6340 or www.fpanet.net. Another place to find a fee-only financial advisor is the National Association of Personal Financial Advisors at www.napfa.org or 800-366-2732. Finally, many accountants also offer financial planning services. To find one, contact the American Institute of Certified Public Accountants: www.aicpa.org or 212-596-6200.

In my first book, *Investing Success: How to Conquer 30 Costly Mistakes & Multiply Your Wealth!* I told readers about the importance of having SMART goals. I also explained that people who set written goals overwhelmingly fare better than those who do not.

Consider Your Short, Medium and Long-Range Goals

I'd like to guide your thinking now toward short-term, medium-range, and long-term goals that you may want to pursue. Short-term goals are those you can accomplish in one or two years at most. Medium-range goals will take two to 10 years to achieve. And long-term goals require you to save or invest for a decade or longer. Here are some goals to which you might aspire:

- Paying off student loans
- Eliminating credit card debt
- Building up an emergency cash cushion
- Buying a new car or a second automobile
- Starting a business
- Saving for a down-payment on a house
- Investing in the stock market or in real estate
- Retiring comfortably

Your Retirement Aspirations

Financial advisors say one of the most frequently asked questions from their clients is: Am I financially prepared for retirement? Yet far fewer people take time to ponder another, equally pressing query: Am I *emotionally* ready to retire?

Certainly, leaving the full-time workforce has serious financial implications. But too often, experts say, economic issues overshadow important emotional considerations.

So if you're planning for your Golden Years, do take time to enhance your retirement I.Q. – ensuring, among other things, that you'll have a healthy-sized nest egg.

But before you retire, don't forget to boost your retirement E.Q. (Emotional Quotient) as well. To ease into retirement with a lot more peace of mind, consider these three questions now – before you bid Corporate America farewell.

- Where do you plan to live?

If you still have a mortgage, or if you plan to purchase another home, this is clearly a financial issue – especially since housing prices vary wildly nationwide. But where you will live during retirement is also an emotionally-laden topic, particularly for couples. Often times, one partner may envision selling the house, moving out of state, or relocating to a warm climate. Meanwhile, the other partner may be sentimentally attached to the family home, may be wary of leaving the current neighborhood, or – far from desiring tropical weather – may want to move closer to the grandchildren in Minneapolis or Buffalo. Thus, talking beforehand with your spouse about these potential areas of disagreement can go a long way toward avoiding future conflicts.

- How will you spend your time?

Figuring out what do with the rest of your life will require some serious soul-searching. It's also important to debunk some myths about what retirement represents.

"A lot of people are afraid of what their lives will be like," says Jerry Kleiman, a clinical psychologist in Long Island, NY. "They associate retirement with diminished capacity, diminished usefulness in society, dependency, or being a step closer to death."

As a result, many people simply stop working and then ask "O.K. now what?"

Kleiman, who is also co-founder of Optimal Resolutions Inc., a consultancy that aids individuals and families with the emotional issues surrounding retirement, suggests that pre-retirees take a "life inventory." This requires you to identify unfulfilled dreams or goals, examine the hobbies and activities that excite you most, and determine what you are passionate about, in terms of intellectual, physical, social or spiritual pursuits.

Similarly, it's also crucial to realize what you *don't* want to do.

"I know some people who want to retire on a beach, and sit around and play cards all day. If I did that, I'd be dead within a year from boredom," says Mark Wachs, a publicist in New York. Wachs, 60, has been meeting with his financial planner recently to prepare for his retirement – a period he views as "the next phase" in his life.

- If your finances fall short of your expectations, can you cope with that reality?

Many of us have grown up with grandiose images of what retirement will be like: freedom from the stresses of work, time to travel, care-free days spent playing golf, or even doing absolutely nothing at all. Unfortunately, these images are more fiction than fact. The average American is woefully unprepared for the financial challenges of life without a steady paycheck – and thus unprepared to deal with the emotional letdown that inevitably occurs when retirement dreams and goals aren't realized.

One big shock for many people is that they probably won't be retiring at all – at least not as soon as, or in the manner, they'd hoped. Ivan Geffen, an investment specialist at Vfinance Investments in Boca Raton, Fla., predicts a lot more retirees will continue to work part-time. Others, he says, will be forced to adopt a less expensive lifestyle.

"With the stock market getting annihilated," between 2000 and 2002 "people's original retirement plans may have to be postponed," Geffen says.

By getting your debts under control now, you can avoid that postponed or "delayed" retirement scenario – and ease into your Golden Years with Zero Debt and maximum financial freedom.

Week Number 3

This week you will:

- Figure out where you will get $ to pay off debt
- Scrutinize your spending
- Make a realistic budget
- Find 10 ways to cut your spending
- Adopt 5 lifestyle changes to save money
- Adjust your W4 withholdings if you get a refund
- Sell or donate stuff you don't need or want

Day 15 Figure out the $69,000 question:
Where will you get the money to pay for your goals, such as slashing your debt?

There are many potential sources of funds you can tap in order to pay down your debts or fund other goals.

Write out this list of possible cash sources:

- Salary/Wages
- Self Employment Income
- Tips
- Second Job
- Inheritance/Gifts
- Borrowed Money (from a bank or family)
- Alimony
- Pension
- Social Security
- Savings
- Investments
- Sell Goods Owned (car, furniture, etc.).

Now, next to each of these items, write one of the following letter codes, based on your chances of getting cash from each source: Write V for Very Likely; P for Possible; NL for Not Likely; and I for Impossible. This is a practical look at your options. Start to consider your circumstances realistically, and think about if you have any other unique sources of funding that you might tap.

Day 16 Scrutinize your spending.

The average U.S. household spends $1.22 for every $1 it earns. That's a recipe for a lifetime of debt. Yet so many of us spend well beyond our means. This is an area I know about all too well, because for many years I was a very big spender. That's a part of my life and personality that I have to carefully manage even now.

How I Got Out of $100,000 in Credit Card Debt

I count myself very fortunate. I once had just over $100,000 in credit card debt, and now I have Zero Debt. When I say I have Zero Debt, I should clarify that: I no longer have any credit card bills – the worse form of "bad" debt. I still have a mortgage and a home equity line of credit. I also still have a small amount of student loans from graduate school. All are at interest rates below 6%. Mortgage debt and college financing are "good" debt. A home is the foundation for wealth building and can be leveraged for investment purposes. Debt associated with your home has tax advantages as well. My graduate school education at the University of Southern California – even the loans that financed my Master of Arts degree from USC – represented an investment in my future. Having an advanced degree has afforded me greater earnings over the years.

With regard to my $100,000-plus credit card debt, though, I am pleased to say that I have paid off everything I owed to creditors. What may be even more startling to most people is that I paid my debts without credit counseling, without enrolling in any debt management program, and without resorting to bankruptcy. What I did do was educate myself, read the fine print on my agreements, and get smart about my use of credit. I was also lucky, very lucky, that I didn't get a single negative mark on my credit file even when I had so much debt.

Ultimately, I paid what I owed – in full and with interest. The interest I shelled out – many thousands of dollars – was the price I paid for overspending and racking up debt year after year.

Being In Debt Denial

When I reflect on my debt, I realize now I was very much in denial. I definitely had a debt problem for years. But I was one of those people who would never admit it. After all, I was a financial journalist. I knew a lot about making money, saving it, and investing it. In fact, I was doing a lot of the right things economically – like socking away pre-tax earnings in my 401(k) every year, putting aside money for my kids' college education, protecting my family with life insurance, and so on. To top it off, I had a nice six-figure salary. So in my head, the fact that I'd amassed this huge $100,000 in debt was somehow O.K. Of course, I know now that it was anything but O.K.

I ran up large amounts of debts in several ways. First, I made poor choices with my money mainly in that my family lived a lifestyle that, in truth, exceeded our income level. We traveled whenever we wanted to, frequently bought gifts and gave money to people, paid for private school for my children, purchased any kind of electronics or gadgets we wanted, and so forth. I was never the woman you'd catch in the mall every week, however. And because I wasn't spending largely on myself – that is, for personal things that women often spend money on – I somehow rationalized that the things I was buying were the things my family *needed*. The reality is that it was just stuff we *wanted*.

Living beyond our means caused us to also use credit to pay for our normal monthly bills from time to time. But a big chunk of my credit card debt came, believe it or not, from a single big-ticket purchase. In 2001, I bought two plots of land for $37,500 at a city auction. My plan was to quickly build a few multi-family homes on the land, sell the properties and net $150,000 bucks. To acquire the land quickly, I didn't bother with getting bank financing or a construction loan. Instead, I just got cash advances from my credit cards and those handy checks that credit card companies sent me month after month. I figured any financing charges I paid would ultimately be worth it. I even convinced myself that I "owned" the land outright – simply because no bank held a mortgage on the property. Well, it's true that I was the owner, on paper, but it was the credit cards that really financed the purchase.

To make a long story short, the "quick" real estate deal I envisioned never happened. But the debt remained.

Downsizing Hits Home

In early 2003, I lost my six-figure television job as a *Wall Street Journal* reporter for CNBC. Like millions of others in Corporate America, I too was laid off in a cost-cutting move. (Remember the five Dreaded D's – Downsizing, Death, Divorce,

Disability and Disease – that I told you could throw your finances awry or exacerbate existing problems?)

Even after my layoff, I didn't reign in my spending. In fact, my spending increased dramatically because I launched my own business and spent $100,000 funding it in 2003. This time, though, I primarily used my savings. It wasn't until this year (2004) that I paid off the last of all my debts in full thanks to – can you guess? – that real estate investment I made back in 2001. Turns out buying the land was a smart investment after all, just not in a way that I'd ever imagined. I never built a thing on it. But the land alone shot up in value and I received $200,000 for it from a cash buyer – more than five times what I paid for it.

So, yes, I'm a Zero Debt convert now, a zealot you might say. But to get here, I've paid a high price for over-spending and for racking up large amounts of debts in the past. For instance, because I wasn't really adding to my debts in 2003 and 2004, I tapped other forms of available funds – and in my case it was hard-earned savings. I took $80,000, for example, out of my 401(k) plan – a money mistake I'd never advise anyone else to do.

I tell you my story in the hopes that you won't be ashamed of the money mistakes you've made. I also want you to know that you're not alone in your debt woes, and that no matter how bad it seems, there is always a way out.

I also reveal my story because I want you to take an honest look at your own spending patterns. The coaching sessions I do with individuals, and the "Get Financially Fit Now!" group workshops I conduct are designed to help people jumpstart their finances and learn to manage their money. In the workshops, I often ask people to distinguish between things that are "luxuries" and things that are "necessities." Invariably, one person will cite some thing – be it a good or a service – as a "necessity" that another person believes is a "luxury."

I then encourage people to gain some perspective on their spending by considering those things that, to them, may seem like necessities, but that to others appear more like luxuries, or even frivolous or downright wasteful spending.

For example, I once told a group of workshop participants that I spend about $300 a month on books. Some attendees were mortified! They gave me all kinds of suggestions (good ones, in fact), about how I could definitely save money by checking out books from the library, reading books in the bookstore, or sharing books with friends, etc. Most people clearly saw my monthly book-buying binge as a luxury – if not a wasteful use of my money – whereas I saw it as a "necessity."

You'd be surprised at how others might see your spending habits. And because I think some outside perspective can be a big eye-opener, I'd like you to take a moment to do the following exercise.

Gaining Perspective on Your Spending

What's a luxury? What is frivolous? What is wasteful?

Directions: Take a few moments by yourself to complete the following statements, filling in the appropriate info. Think about things you spend money on that you consider "necessities" but that outsiders might not view that way.

I now spend $ _____ weekly/monthly/yearly on _____
something some people may consider a luxury.

I also spend $ _____ weekly/monthly/yearly on _____
which other people might view as frivolous.

Furthermore, I spend $__a week/month/year on _____
which certain people could think is wasteful.

Now go ask a family member or friend to read aloud your statements. Then ask him/her to honestly answer 3 questions:

1. Do you think any of the things I am spending money on are "luxuries," "frivolous," or "wasteful?"
2. Why or why not?
3. Is there a better way for me to eliminate or reduce these expenses?

After you receive some feedback, put one or two recommendations from relatives or friends into practice if they make sense and if the advice will save you money.

Day 17 Make a *realistic* budget.

If you've read this far into *Zero Debt*, I have to assume that you're not just a casual reader – you've likely had your fair share of money woes. Well, I'm a firm believer that when most people experience cash-flow problems, it's usually caused by one of two things:

Causes Of Cash Flow Problems

1) You *Don't* Have A Budget .... Or
2) You *Do* Have A Budget ... *But* ...

It gets blown by that dirty, rotten **S.C.U.M.**

What is SCUM? Let me tell you right away that it's not: "Some Cousin, Uncle or Mama" – although you may feel like certain relatives are draining you financially!

Fill in the blanks below ... SCUM actually stands for "Something Came Up Monthly."

S_____

C_____

U_____

M_____

How many times have you thought your were getting ahead on your bills, only to have something "come up" that you didn't anticipate? It could be that you loan money to a friend in need;

someone in the family gets sick; your kid's school has a fund-raising drive – whatever. The end result is always the same: some unexpected expense fouls up your budget.

Now for some people, the real problem is that they've never truly created a written budget at all. They just spend willy-nilly and hope that checks don't bounce.

But even those people who actually do make budgets seem to constantly blow their budgets.

4 Simple Steps To Stop Blowing Your Budget

In fact, each month, millions of Americans dutifully plan their household budgets – only to have some unforeseen event come along and totally wreck what are seemingly well-made financial plans.

If you ask most of these people how their budgets went awry, the response will almost invariably be: "Something came up," followed by an explanation about how their house roof leaked, their car conked out, or someone in the family unexpectedly took ill.

While unanticipated situations can certainly spoil even the best-laid economic plans, why is it that many individuals blow their budgets month after month after month? In my many years of talking to consumers, financial counselors and money management experts, I've come to the conclusion that true "emergencies" – like those described above – actually happen relatively infrequently. So while most people *think* they run out of money because some emergency "came up," the reality is that most people blow their budgets because **LIFE** happened to them.

LIFE is an acronym that describes the four ways that your budget gets out of whack – forcing you to spend more than you planned for the month, or causing you to live from paycheck to paycheck.

- Listed items are under-calculated.

The "L" in LIFE stands for expenses that are "Listed" items in your budget, but your numbers are actually way off the mark. Unfortunately, many individuals who draw up budgets don't use very precise numbers. People have a tendency to underestimate their spending. Take cellular phones for example. If you own one, you probably account for it in your monthly budget with a figure like $49.99 – or whatever your basic monthly charge happens to be. But do you find that you regularly talk beyond your allotted cell phone minutes, so that you wind up with a mobile phone bill closer to $80 per month? If so, you need to adjust your budget and put in more realistic numbers for this expense. Household bills, like electricity and gas, are another area where people get tripped up. They include these expenses as a flat cost in their budgets, say $100 a month. But their heating or air conditioning bill is routinely far more than that $100, especially during times of extreme weather.

- Impulse purchases seduce you.

We all make impulse purchases from time to time – but some people do it on a regular basis. It may be that you're reading the newspaper and you see a discount coupon for a retail store you like. And before long, you're at the mall shopping. Other times, you may be surfing the Internet looking for information, when a pop-up ad seduces you with some intriguing advertisement. Next thing you know, you've whipped out your credit card to buy some product or service.

- Forgotten bills surface.

Some bills get paid annually or perhaps twice a year. If you're not careful in your planning, you can exclude these expenses from your budget and then when the bills come due you realize you forgot all about them. Has this ever happened to you? If so, don't omit from your budget those expenditures that may not be paid on a monthly basis – things like your homeowner's or auto insurance, the maintenance fee for the vacation time share you own, your gym membership, or any annual fees you pay to belong to personal, professional or civic organizations.

- Emergency or unexpected events occur.

Lastly, there are obviously times when emergencies – like a burst boiler unit – can ruin a budget. Try to minimize these events with preventative measures, such as regularly servicing your boiler, having routine maintenance done on your car to avoid breakdowns, and making periodic visits to the doctor to stave off serious medical conditions.

Once you realize that LIFE happens to everyone, you can take some steps to safeguard your budget. Start by reviewing your finances and taking a hard, realistic look at your overall spending habits. If you've been vastly under-calculating listed items in your budget, make the necessary adjustments. If you make too many impulse purchases, carry less cash with you or put your credit cards away to minimize the temptation to buy on a whim. Take a half hour to fine-tune your budget and make sure you haven't forgotten any one-off bills. Additionally, consider what you can do to reduce those "emergency" situations – especially the kind that can be cured with a little preventive medicine. Lastly, think very hard about your own budget busters.

Listed items were under-calculated
Impulse buying
Forgotten bills
Emergencies or unexpected expenses

Now list some of your budget busters below. Place a letter – L, I, F, or E – next to each one. Do you see any patterns?

What are your budget busters?

L   I   F   E

1. _____

2. _____

3. _____

4. _____

Day 18 Find 10 ways to cut your spending.

Today I want you to come up with 10 ways to cut your spending. Don't complain about it or say it's impossible. Just put your thinking cap on and get busy. If you really had to – and at this point, you *do* really have to in order to eliminate your money problems – I'm sure you could be really creative.

But just to jumpstart your thinking, I'll start you out with 10 ideas:

- Do your own home maintenance
- Only go to your bank's ATMs
- Bring lunch to work daily or a few days a week
- Visit www.lowermybills.com to save on 18 types of bills
- Stop smoking (or drinking)
- Carpool
- Use coupons (always or from time to time)
- Buy in bulk
- Raise your insurance deductibles
- Plan and pay for travel in advance

Saving Money Doesn't Have To Be A Big Hassle

I'm constantly amazed at how many people pay full price for products and services – when they could so readily get the things they need for a lot less money.

For many consumers, though, the idea of saving big bucks on everything from soap and toilet paper to a new car or medical insurance means either hours of coupon clipping and haggling with salesmen. Neither tactic is especially attractive for busy people who have family, career and other demands on their time.

Thankfully, there are some fast, painless and – dare I say it? – *fun* ways to save money, simply by hopping on the Internet. After all, who doesn't relish snagging a true bargain?

Take your homeowner's or auto insurance. To save money there, check out www.lowermybills.com. They comparison shop for you and get you the best insurance rates. Since homeowner's coverage averages $603 a year in 2004 and auto insurance another $855, according to the Insurance Information Institute, if you spend 20 minutes surfing the web to save 10% on these insurance expenses, you can readily put $145 back into your bank account.

And don't forget to look for ways to curb costs on big-ticket items, such as your mortgage or car note. If you want to slash the amount of money you're doling out for your monthly car payment, it's well worth it to visit www.capitaloneauto.com. They let you refinance your existing auto loan. Typical time it takes to fill out the application: 10 minutes. Average savings: $404 per year, and $1,353 over the life of the car loan.

If you're a person who gets into a grocery or clothing store and loses your mind, buying indiscriminately and not getting a lot of value for your hard-earned money, get some help from the experts at www.thefrugalshopper.com. This site also gives you great tips on how to save money on a variety of products and services. (Yes, they tell you to use coupons – but that's just one strategy!)

Day 19 Adopt five lifestyle changes as strategies to save more money.

Have you ever thought about how making small changes in the way to live can actually save you loads of money? Well, today I'd like you to think about your lifestyle and what areas might be out of whack with your current desires to become financially free – and achieve Zero Debt status.

For example, do you live in a metropolitan area and take cabs too frequently – instead of hopping aboard the less expensive subway or rail system?

Do you entertain once a month or more at your home – I'm not talking lavish parties, but certainly large enough or frequent enough shindigs (or even pizza and beer bashes!) that you have to dole out a lot of money for food and drinks, etc.?

Do you think you're "above" wearing clothes that don't carry a designer label?

Maybe none of these situations describes your lifestyle. That's fine. I still want you to think about how it is that you're living.

We all have areas of our life that, with minor adjustments, we can save money. My goal here isn't to send you into "can't have" or "can't do" mode. I simply want you to consider less-expensive options, or alternatives to what you may be currently doing.

Again, to get you going, here are five lifestyle changes from which I think most people could benefit:

When shopping, never pay full retail price

That's right, I said NEVER pay full retail. You might be thinking, "How is that even possible?" Well, for starters, you can wait for the item to go on sale, you could find equivalent bargains online, you might also hit outlets or discount stores, or you can simply say: "I don't need/want it *that* badly" – and walk away. (For those of you with a shopping Jones, please read the special advice at the end of this chapter called "How To Look Like a Million Bucks Without Spending a Fortune.")

Become a frequent library patron

Borrow videos, DVDs and books instead of purchasing them. The average DVD is now $20. If you buy 10 a year – and many households actually have dozens in their collections – you'll save hundreds of dollars.

Take advantage of free/low-cost attractions and events in your city

Enjoy parades, museums, and city parks rather than expensive outings like amusement parks.

Eat out less often

Saving $5 a day by skipping fast food or restaurants will keep $1,825 a year in your pocket; $10 a day means an annual savings of $3,650.

Walk, instead of driving, to any place that's within walking distance

You'll save money on gas, help the environment, and be healthier too!

My point is that there are probably some behavioral patterns in your life – some things that you do frequently, buy regularly or spend money on all the time – that may not be financially feasible or prudent at this time. If so, see if you can change those things. And who knows: After a few months, you might even find that you *enjoy* the lifestyle adjustments. One thing is certain: you'll have a fatter bank account to show for your actions.

On the following pages, you'll find a special chapter supplement for all you serious shopaholics out there – guys and gals! This information was included in my first book, *Investing Success*, because I realize there are so many people out there who feel financially pinched because of their spending habits. So if you've got too many bills to pay, and a little less cash than you'd like to go around, try the following ideas. They represent my Top 10 Rules for Money-Wise Shoppers.

How to Look Like a Million Bucks (Without Spending a Fortune)

1.   **Never pay full retail price. Ever.**
I'm not suggesting that you walk into Barney's, or even your local department store, and start haggling over prices. But any savvy fashion editor or stylist will tell you that nobody (in the know) pays the full asking price for anything these days. Here are a few pointers:

- For starters, you can *wait until the item goes on sale* (trust me, it will!)
- *Shop sample sales* in major cities and get designer duds for a fraction of the retail price. These to-die-for sales usually happen after Fashion Week in New York, Los Angeles, London, Milan and Paris
- *Buy classic styles off-season*. Great pieces look good season to season.
- *Hop online*. All of these web sites sell designer merchandise both in an off-season: decadestwo.com (for vintage chic); yoox.com, (for Italian designers); bluefly.com; and ebay.com (yes, ebay! It offers high-end designer clothes, including some that hit the Net before they're available nationally); overstock.com; and starwares.com (for celebrity duds).
- *Think Outlets, Outlets, Outlets*. The book *Buying Retail Is Stupid! The National Discount Guide to Buying Everything at up to 80% Off Retail,* written by Trisha King and Deborah Newmark, offers state-by-state listings of factory outlets. Last time I checked, this comprehensive, 396-page guide, could be bought on Amazon.com for just $2.55.
- Finally, *you can actually negotiate* in many boutiques and specialty stores. Don't be obnoxious about it. But when you find something you want, just sort of wrinkle your nose up a bit and, while holding the price tag, ever-so-nicely ask the sales person: "$75? Is that the best price you can offer me?"

2.   **Don't shop another day until you organize your closet.**
In your head, you may think you *need* another black skirt. But you probably just *want* one, because if you carefully go through your closet (that's right, sort out all those folded piles and even the stuff in bags and tucked away in the corners), you'll probably find that you have at least two or three – and likely even more – perfectly fine black skirts. So it's hard to justify buying yet another black skirt under these

circumstances. By organizing your closet, you'll also be far less prone to making impulse purchases of other things you mistakenly believe you "need."

3. Think like a celebrity.
When you see Halle Berry or Jennifer Lopez donning a gorgeous dress, wearing Harry Winston jewels or even sporting a sexy pair of Jimmy Choo shoes, *realize that they rarely pay for these clothes and accessories*. In fact, designers shower them with goods knowing that having these A-list celebrities wear their clothes will be good publicity and thus boost sales. The celebs themselves more often than not will wear the item once (if the designer is lucky). But then that item gets donated to charity or tossed in the back of what I'm sure is the world's largest walk-in closet. In any event, consider this: Since multi-millionaire "superstars" aren't even paying to look like stars, why should you? If you keep in mind that a $1,000 dress you're pining away for is probably only realistically going to be worn by you just once (like the stars do), chances are you may be willing to forego splurging on that item if you can't really afford it.

4. Take a friend shopping.
And I don't mean your girlfriend whose Visa bill is constantly more than her rent. I'm talking about your level headed friend, the one who doesn't call you every other week to borrow money because her paycheck has run out. One suggestion though: don't drag along a pal (however well-intentioned) who simply can't have fun on your shopping quest. Instead, bring along your "I-know-how-to-enjoy-myself-too-but-I'm-not-going-to-squander-my-rent-payment-to-do-it" buddy. What's the point of all this? A friend with a good head on her shoulders will keep you from making outlandish purchases and wasting your money. She'll make you accountable for your spending actions. And accountability counts.

5. Establish a pre-set limit before you go shopping.
Just come up with a ballpark figure (say $500) and let that serve as your cap. Now here's where you get to enjoy yourself – and not feel deprived. Mentally allow yourself the option of going 10% over your pre-set limit. So if you absolutely CAN'T do without a $50 bra and panties set, but you've already reached your $500 limit, you can go ahead and make the purchase, and do so guilt-free. Any spending beyond that, though, and you're asking for trouble. This way, if you stick to your pre-set limit, you'll be patting yourself on the back. If you go as high as your spending-cap-plus-10% limit, at least you've still

138

stayed within the guidelines, without breaking the bank. Bonus: if you actually spend 10% under, celebrate! One caveat: don't spend the 10% you saved (and then some) on an expensive dinner or some other one-time event. Instead, sock that money away into a "hands-off" savings account.

6. Go where the real bargains are.

Serious fashionistas who can swing it go to London or Milan for fashion bargains. The cost of the airplane ticket can be well worth it if you pick up, say, Italian boots for $100 that you'd spend $450 for in the U.S. You'd obviously only use this strategy when you're planning to buy multiple items for which the savings alone would pay for the cost of your travel.

7. Frequent discount retailers.

Pick up the trendiest looks at stores like Target and H&M. Don't worry that the clothes didn't come from a so-called upscale retailer. Most times, no one will know the difference.

8. Make mental comparisons.

When you are tempted to plop down a big chunk of money for, say, a cashmere sweater (and yes, I know it's a beautiful one), ask yourself: is this *really* worth a full day's pay? For more expensive items think: is this truly worth a week (or whatever time) of my labor?

9. Do something radical.

If you find yourself at the mall every week (or even every day), plan to make a radical change – if only temporarily. Make a vow to do ABSOLUTELY no shopping whatsoever for an entire month, or for whatever period of time you think you can stand it. You'd be surprised how much strength you can muster up if you put your mind to it. And while you're saving gobs of money in the process, you'll find other creative uses of your time – and cash.

10. Give something away.

Emulate your favorite celebrity and make a donation to a worthwhile cause. Surely you have something in the back of your closet or packed away in the attic or basement that you've not worn in a month's worth of Sundays. Give it to a charity or a woman's shelter. There's truth in the saying: What goes around, comes around. You give something to someone else in need, and your generosity will come back to you in some way. In other words: to get a blessing, first *be* a blessing!

Day 20 At work, adjust your W-4 withholdings if you receive a refund.

The IRS says that the average tax refund mailed in early 2004 was nearly $2,300. If you always get money back from Uncle Sam, it means you're giving the government an interest-free loan.

Refund Checks Show Poor Financial Planning

I don't care how much you enjoy getting that "bonus" once a year. Generally speaking, any time you get a federal tax refund, that demonstrates that there was a lack of proper financial planning on your part. Getting a big refund – no matter how good it feels at the time – isn't smart and it doesn't make sense. Instead of letting the feds take out extra taxes, keep your money and use it wisely.

A Quick Fix Via Your Human Resources Department

Go to your HR department at work and adjust your W4 withholdings so that your employer takes out less taxes from your paycheck. Your next paycheck will be bigger. Use the extra money to pay down your debt. When you raise your number of withholdings, make sure that you track your level of taxes paid. Don't take out too few taxes and wind up with a big tax bill April 15th. But if you owe a small amount to the government, that's better than getting a refund; it means you had more cash the previous year.

Day 21 Sell or donate stuff you don't want, use or need.

Want to raise some extra cash in a hurry? Hold a yard sale and unload unwanted electronics, clothing, furniture or other household goods. Get rid of anything you don't want, need or use regularly. These items can also be auctioned on eBay (www.ebay.com). When you get the money from your sales, send it to your creditors to pay down your debt. You can also donate most goods to charity, get a receipt for your contribution, and reap a tax break for your generosity.

Holiday Giving All Year Round

November and December tend to be the months of the year when many people turn their thoughts to charitable giving. However, you don't have to wait until year's end to be generous. But scores of citizens don't get the tax breaks they deserve from their philanthropic efforts simply because they vastly underestimate the value of their donations – or they're among the 80 million Americans who don't itemize their deductions, and therefore can't claim charitable contributions on their federal tax returns.

But with just a little bit of work, you can reap big financial benefits from your generosity.

For many givers, the key is to correctly calculate the total value of your charitable largesse – whether it's cash, or figuring out the worth of a couch, computer monitor, or a man's suit donated to charity.

Here are five suggestions to get the most out of your charitable giving. You may not have big chunks of cash to donate to organizations like the Salvation Army or Red Cross. But if you donate any non-cash items – like clothes, toys, or household goods – you need to figure out the cash value of those items. The IRS isn't known for having simple rules and codes. But this is one area where Uncle Sam is very clear: you can deduct the going price for an item based on its condition at the time you donate it.

* One way to value your donations is to find out what a local thrift shop or consignment store charges for similar items.

* You can also look at the classified ads in your local newspaper for the price of a similar product. Again, you'll need to take into consideration the condition of your donation. If you're giving a fairly new coat that's in excellent condition, you could adjust the value upward from what others are charging.

* Finally, if you'd rather not call up thrift stores or go through classified listings, you can use a software program, such as ItsDeductible, which has already surveyed average prices nationwide. The ItsDeductible software, owned by Intuit (www.intuit.com), determines and assigns accurate valuations to thousands of commonly donated items. This way, there's no guesswork in valuing your donations – and you can have confidence that you're not overstating the value of your donations. Neither would you be shortchanging yourself by taking deductions that are too modest, as most people do.

The folks at Intuit are so confident that you'll get big returns by using their software that they guarantee that ItsDeductible will save you at least $300 in taxes.

You'd probably be surprised to know what you can legitimately claim for items in good condition that you donate to charity. For example, a computer monitor is valued at $107, a man's designer two-piece suit $399, a girl's casual dress $8, a silk tie $26, and a pullover sweater $21, according to ItsDeductible.

* For additional information, get a copy of IRS publication 561, called Determining the Value of Donated Property. You can also call the IRS at 1-800-TAX-FORM and request a free copy of this publication.

* You should always have records to back up your estimates.

For any contribution under $250, keep a receipt from the charity, or your own written record of the donation. It should show the charity's name and address, the date and location of the donation, a description of what you donated, its market value, and the original cost.

If you give something valued above $250, you should have a letter or written acknowledgement from the charity documenting the specifics of your donation, and spelling out any good or services you may have received in exchange for your contribution. For items valued between $501 and $5,000, you should also be prepared, if necessary, to show the IRS records indicating how you originally obtained the property (whether it was a gift, purchase, or inheritance), its original cost, and the approximate date that you obtained the property.

Week Number 4

This week you will:

- Find a way to generate additional income
- Apply for a home equity loan or line of credit
- Refinance your auto loan
- Pick a "Pay Down Your Debt" priority strategy
- Consider the pros and cons of debt management programs
- Evaluate your existing insurance coverage
- Draw up a will

Day 22 Find a way to generate additional income.

Anything you can do to generate other income can go a long way towards reducing your debt – especially if you'd like to wipe out your bills fast. One option is to get a second job, even if only temporarily.

Is a Second Job, or Part-Time Work In Your Future?

I realize that most people already work really hard, and often put in more than 40 hours a week on the job. But if you can even fathom the idea, consider getting a second job or part-time work – just for a set period of time, perhaps three months. This may seem like a big sacrifice and a burden. But trust me: it's nothing compared to the burden of carrying around debt year after year. Take every dollar earned from your second job and use it to reduce debt or build an emergency savings fund.

Your emergency fund, or emergency cash cushion, should be at least three times your monthly expenses. In other words, if your bills are $3,000 a month, you should have a $9,000 emergency fund. I know this is hard to amass, but you can build it over time. And trust me, having a cash cushion is crucial in case one of the 5 Dreaded D's (downsizing, death, divorce, disability or disease) ever happens to you.

Turn a Hobby Into Cash

Maybe right now you're saying: "Lynnette, you have absolutely lost your mind if you think I'm going to go slaving away on a job for even more hours than I do now!"

Well, if the idea of more *work* is so unbearable, how about *playing* for money? And I don't mean hitting the slots or the crap tables in Vegas or Atlantic City. I mean do you have any hobbies – or things you do for fun or entertainment – that you can actually turn into cold, hard dollars?

Like to knit or sew things? There's a market for that – just go after people who might want hand-made (read: customized or tailored) clothing. Charge your customers enough to cover all your expenses, for fabric, supplies, etc. Then add in a hefty labor charge to make it worth your while.

Perhaps you're good at styling or cutting people's hair and you actually like to be creative in that way as well. OK, so put the word out in your neighborhood, or among your family and friends, that you'll do hair – for a fee – from the comfort of your home.

Whatever pass-time you take pleasure in, chances are there's someone out there willing to pay you for it – regardless of whether or not you're providing goods or service.

The Small-Office Home-Office Solution

Speaking of goods and services, now may be the time to consider doing something that so many Americans are angling to do: start their own business. And if millions of entrepreneurs across the country are correct, one of the best ways to launch a business is right out of your own home (or apartment ... or garage).

The Ideal Part-Time Enterprise

A word to you dreamers out there: Don't look at this advice and go off half-cocked talking to your spouse about how you're going to start raising ostriches and make $100,000 a year at it – and I don't care if you happen to live on a farm! In all cases, you want to hone in on no-cost or low-cost ventures; businesses that you can do by yourself, and if possible, start-ups that can be operated exclusively or mainly from the privacy of your own home.

Why these characteristics? For starters, you don't have the money to buy tons of products. You also don't want to have to hire anybody. Hey, you need to keep all the money you'll earn, don't you? And by taking the home-based approach, you won't have to pay extra money to lease space or rent a place from which you'll run your home-based business (you're already paying something to live where you are, right?). Running the business from home also means no commuting costs or commuting time (unless you call the 30-second walk from your bedroom to your basement a serious commute).

Leverage The Internet

Finally, if you're a person who is web savvy, I'd encourage you by all means to harness the power of the Internet to make money in any way possible – any way that's legal and moral, of course. For instance, maybe you're a good writer. Scores of corporations and organizations out there need writers to – well, write – all kinds of stuff: pamphlets, brochures, company newsletters, employment manuals, etc.

You can offer to do desktop publishing services if you have a penchant for that. Perhaps you speak another language: think about selling online language instruction. With the World Wide Web as your gateway, your customer base is almost unlimited. Clients can be in any parts of the world – as long as they're willing to hire you and pay up in a timely manner.

If you follow these guidelines, and are willing to think creatively about how you can pad your current income – without killing yourself in the process – you can slash your debts by leaps and bounds and become financially fit much, much faster.

Day 23 Apply for a home equity loan or equity line of credit.

If you have equity in your house, it can be a wise strategy to use a home equity loan to pay off your credit card debt. One helpful source: Countrywide Financial, the largest mortgage lender in the United States. Visit the company online at www.countrywide.com or call 800-556-9568. The interest you pay on mortgage debt is tax-deductible up to $100,000 and mortgages typically carry much lower interest rates than credit card debt. But caution: don't pay off those credit card bills, and put your home at risk with an equity loan if you're just going to go back out and run up your charge cards again.

The decision to take out a home equity loan is one that should not be made lightly. I've heard heart-breaking stories of people who paid off their credit card debts by converting those obligations into mortgage debt – only to keep spending, not change their financial habits, and wind up losing their homes in foreclosure. I don't want this to happen to you.

Home ownership is critical to your financial security. For more than 90% of all millionaires in the U.S., real estate is a cornerstone of their wealth. Owning real estate – either your principal residence and/or investment property – has terrific financial advantages. You get tax breaks for paying property taxes and mortgage interest. You get regular income and can take a depreciation deduction for rental property. If you have a home-based business, the tax breaks are even juicier; Uncle Sam lets you write off a variety of expenses associated with running your business from the comfort of your abode.

As a homeowner, you also get the chance to enjoy price appreciation, something that's happened to most residential real estate throughout the country in recent years. U.S. Census Data show that the average sales price of a single-family home jumped by 56% since 1995 to $244,800 at the end of 2003.

For these reasons and more, you've probably heard it said that renting an apartment is simply "throwing your money away" month after month. I believe that it's actually worse than that. It's not just that you're not reaping a multitude of financial incentives. Renting a home or an apartment puts you at a big disadvantage in other ways. Home ownership often affords you right and freedoms renters don't have. For instance, you can paint the inside of your house any color you want, hang paintings on the wall wherever you'd like, or have a cat or dog if you so choose. If you're renting, though, you have to get a landlord's permission to do these things – not always an easy task. Home ownership also has considerable intangible benefits – like the pride you get from being a homeowner (don't you love it when visitors compliment you on your beautiful garden?) or the sense of satisfaction you feel just knowing you're setting a good example for young people and others who aspire to home ownership. Lastly, a home provides more than just a roof over your head each night or a meeting place for family gatherings. It can become part of your legacy – an asset that you own free and clear and perhaps leave to your children or grandchildren.

Unfortunately, too many people are using up the equity in their homes at unprecedented levels. That worries me greatly. Fifty years ago, Americans averaged about 85% equity in their homes, net of debt. Today that figure is around 57%, according to George Marotta, a NAPFA-registered financial advisor and research fellow at Stanford University's Hoover Institution.

Since housing prices have escalated so dramatically over the past decade, you'd think that Americans would have lots *more* equity in their homes, not a lot *less*. The problem is that people who lack proper money management skills are getting cash-out mortgage refinancing to pay off debts and make various expenditures. My concern is that at some point, many individuals will find themselves in situations where the homes that were keeping them afloat start to sink under a boatload of debts.

What's the Difference Between a Home Equity Loan and a Home Equity Line Of Credit?

Having duly warned you about the perils of tapping your home's equity, let me now reiterate that using mortgage debt to pay off consumer debt – like credit cards and auto loans – can be a smart thing to do. Just make sure your spending patterns and money habits won't get you into financial trouble again. And if you heed the advice contained in *Zero Debt*, you shouldn't have a problem.

To tap the equity in your home, you'll have to decide whether you need a home equity loan or an equity line of credit. An equity loan is best if you require one big lump sum – like to pay off all your debts in one fell swoop. You'll then have to start paying back the entire amount borrowed. With an equity line of credit, you have access to funds, up to your maximum credit available, but you don't pay back any money until you actually use the funds. Also, with an equity line of credit you use checks to draw upon your available credit. When you have those checks, it can be tempting to use them for any number of reasons. But don't make the mistake that so many people do of using your home equity line of credit to pay for your normal monthly bills or your daily living expenses. That's an imprudent use of your home equity, and hazardous to your personal wealth.

Need A Mortgage? Credit Re-Scoring Can Help

If you're applying for a new mortgage or are refinancing and think you may get turned down because of inaccurate, outdated or negative erroneous information on your credit report, make sure you go with a lender who knows about "credit re-scoring."

Here's how it works. If you have a mortgage application pending, and you know there are mistakes in your credit file, your lender (via a third-party rapid re-scoring firm) submits proof of the error to the credit bureaus. Equifax, Experian and TransUnion all have special departments set up to deal with these requests on an expedited basis. After receiving the proper proof of the mistake, the credit bureau updates your credit file. No one *guarantees* that your FICO score will be raised, but experts in the field say most times, it works. Among the types of information that can be corrected are:

- Collection accounts still showing an unpaid status
- Judgments or Tax Liens that have been paid or satisfied
- Payments erroneously reported as late, or changes in account status, such as from "delinquent" to "current"

- Debts that should be included in a discharged bankruptcy
- Accounts that were paid and closed but still show a balance

Only mortgage lenders can initiate the rapid re-scoring process with the credit bureaus. Individuals can't do it. According to Credit Communications Inc., a credit re-scoring firm, the credit bureaus only accept official documents as proof of mistakes, such as:

- A Letter from the creditor or collection agency
  (And it must have the same account number on the letter or receipt as is being reported by the credit bureaus)
- Certified satisfaction of judgment from a court
- Certified tax lien release from the IRS
- Certified bankruptcy discharge papers from a court
- The bureaus will not accept the following documentation: canceled checks, receipts for money orders, account statements, hand-written letters, third party documentation.

The rapid re-scoring process can be a powerful way to quickly improve your credit profile in as little as 48 hours. Again, it's only for those in the market for a mortgage, and the updates are only made when there are errors – not true and correct information – in your credit report.

What Are Reverse Mortgages?

For those of you who are aged 62 and over, another method of freeing up some cash to pay off your credit card debts (and yes, older people have increasing amounts of debt too!) is to consider a reverse mortgage. Here's what a reverse mortgage is and how it can be used to your benefit.

A traditional mortgage represents an obligation on your part, where you pay a monthly payment to a bank or mortgage company over a fixed number of years. The more money you pay, the more equity you build up in the house. After a set time, say 30 years, you own the home outright. A reverse mortgage is still a loan against your house, but it works the opposite way: instead of you paying the bank, the bank pays you a fixed stream of money until you or the last surviving borrower dies or sells the home. The loan the bank provides can be in the form of upfront money and/or regular monthly payments. This loan doesn't have to be repaid for as long as you live in the house. Over time, the more money the bank pays/lends you, the larger your debt becomes. With each payment you collect from the bank, your equity in the house is reduced. A reverse mortgage lender will analyze your situation and tell you how big a loan you'd qualify for, based on your age and your home's value.

To get a reverse mortgage, you must meet these criteria:

- You must be at least 62 years old and living in your home as your main place of residence.
- Your home must be a single-family residence in a 1-to-4 unit building, condominium or part of a planned unit development. Manufactured homes qualify, but most co-ops and mobile homes don't.
- Your home must be at least one year old and meet HUD's property standards. However, if you need the money to pay for required repairs, you can still qualify.

- You must not have any debt against your property. To meet this rule, most people simply get a cash advance from the reverse mortgage and use the money to pay off any existing loans/mortgages against their property.
- You must go through reverse-mortgage counseling to make sure you understand this loan product.

The Pros and Cons Of Reverse Mortgages

As America's retirees and its aging baby boomer population grapple with rising medical costs, retirement portfolios battered by the stock market, and increased personal debt, more and more people are turning to reverse mortgages as a way to have adequate cash flow. But senior citizens and others have lots of misconceptions about reverse mortgages. Perhaps the biggest myth is that you could lose your home. The truth is that you can't. Nor can you wind up owing more than the home is worth; federal law prohibits this. After you die or sell your home, if you had a reverse mortgage, the amount to be paid back to the bank is the total of the payments you received plus interest. Another misconception about these loans is that the borrower gives up ownership of the home. In reality, if you get a reverse mortgage, you keep title and ownership of your house. The bank, however, does get a lien against the property. If you or someone you know is thinking about getting a reverse mortgage, be sure you weigh the following pros and cons. Here are the positive factors concerning reverse mortgages:

- The money can be used for any purpose you want.

- These loans are available in all 50 states, including the District of Columbia and Puerto Rico.
- Income, employment and credit standing are not considerations, since you don't have to repay anything.

Now here are the negative factors concerning reverse mortgages:

- You won't be able to leave the home free and clear for your kids. In most cases, the loan is paid back after the borrower's death by selling the property.
- The cost of getting a reverse mortgage can be quite high. Origination fees can run as much as 2%. Also, mortgage insurance – which is mandatory for these loans – may total another 2%. Expect other fees: title insurance, appraisal etc.

For more information on this topic, check out a publication from the AARP called "Home Made Money: A Consumer's Guide to Reverse Mortgages." You can find it at the organization's web site, www.aarp.com or by calling the AARP membership line at 888-687-2277. The industry's trade group, the National Reverse Mortgage Lenders Association, also has three helpful consumer guides: "Just the FAQs: Answers to Common Questions About Reverse Mortgages;" "Using Reverse Mortgages for Healthcare: An NRMLA Guide;" and "The NRMLA Consumer Guide to Reverse Mortgages." All are free and can be downloaded from the group's web site at www.nrmla.org. You can also contact the NRMLA by telephone at 866-264-4466 to order these informative publications.

Day 24 Refinance your auto loan.

When you're trying to achieve Zero Debt status and financial freedom, you must remember to think about all the types of debts you owe: mortgages, auto loans, credit cards, student loans, etc. Anytime you buy a car, realize that you're purchasing a depreciating asset. Translation: as soon as you drive that new or used vehicle off the dealer's lot, it immediately starts to lose value. Nobody ever re-sells a car for more than they paid for it. That makes a car different from other assets you might buy, like a home or stocks, where your expectation is that you'll later sell them for more than your purchase price. So if you're making car payments, it's especially important that you manage this debt wisely. If you can't pay 100% cash for your new wheels (and most people don't), then at least you can be a savvy consumer when it comes to having an auto loan. Your goal is to save money, and to avoid any negative marks on your credit that can result from missing car payments or having your car repossessed. Fortunately, vehicle financing is one area where you can definitely cut your expenses (and keep the Repo Man at bay) with a little know-how and some simple action.

Many people don't know that you can refinance your car loan, just as you can refinance a mortgage. But a car refinancing is easier, faster and requires no points, appraisal or closing costs. For this reason, auto refinancing has been called "one of the best-kept secrets in personal finance."

To lower your car payments, turn to Capital One Auto Finance (www.capitaloneauto.com), the top online vehicle lender in the United States. Refinancing takes just 15 minutes and saves an average of $1,353 over the life of the loan. What will you do with the money you save? Pay down all your other debts, naturally.

The Capital One Advantage

If you're in the market to buy a new or used car or motorcycle, Capital One Auto also offers you a blank check to buy the vehicle and give you more negotiating power at a car dealership.

Take the case of Jim Adsley. Adsley thought he got a good deal, in late 2001, when he bought a used Cadillac with 8.25% financing through GMAC. But then in 2002, he found an even better bargain, by refinancing his auto loan at a 6.9% rate.

"I'll save about $3,500" over the life of the loan, says Adsley, a retiree from Langley, WA, who used Capital One Auto.

All across the country, scores of consumers like Adsley are refinancing their car loans – prompted by the same low interest rate environment spurring droves of homeowners to refinance their mortgages.

Auto refinancing is happening in much smaller numbers though. In 2003, an estimated 525,000 people refinanced their auto loans, with a combined loan balance of $10 billion, according to CNW Marketing Research. Meanwhile, the Mortgage Bankers Association reports that millions of homeowners refinanced their mortgages in 2003, with those loans totaling nearly $1 trillion.

Still, the number of people who have refinanced car notes is up 100% since 2001, says Matt Coffin, CEO of LowerMyBills.com. The web-based company allows consumers to comparison shop to slash their car payments and other monthly expenses. Coffin notes that one benefit of doing an auto refinancing is that, unlike refinancing a home loan, there are no points to pay and no appraisal required. "So you can save a lot of money," he says.

You generate savings in one of two ways. You can simply refinance your current loan if interest rates are lower than they were when you bought your car. Or you can extend the life of your auto loan, spreading your payments over a longer time period and thereby lowering your monthly car bill. Some people do both.

Online Lenders Dominate Auto Refinancing

Currently, hundreds of lenders nationwide offer auto refinancing. Many are online companies, such as E-loan.com, Bankloan.com and RefinanceFirst.com.

The biggest player in the business though is CapitalOneAuto.com, a unit of Capital One Financial.

At CapitalOneAuto.com, you fill out an online application, providing information about your current monthly car payment, interest rate, and balance due. The company immediately performs a credit check, and if you apply during normal business hours, you receive an e-mail answer within 15 minutes. If you're approved, the message will state your new monthly payment and revised interest rate. (Note: It pays to have good credit: as of July 2004,

CapitalOneAuto.com's best refinance rate was 4.95% for 12-36 month loans and 5.39% for 37-60 month loans). After approval, the company mails you a check to pay off your existing car loan. Then you start making new payments to CapitalOneAuto.com.

For any auto refinancing, you'll pay a lien transfer fee. It runs between $5 and $65, depending on the state in which you live.

Beware Of Extending Your Loan Length

While auto refinancing offers savings and speed, it also has potential downsides if you extend the life of your car loan unnecessarily. For instance, say you bought a car three years ago and originally had a five-year loan. You now have only two years left before you own the vehicle free and clear. But if you refinanced by taking out a new five-year loan, you'd be tacking on another three years of payments – extra interest and all. Additionally, any warranty covering your car could expire before you finish paying off your new loan.

That's why auto refinancing typically makes the most sense for new loans where you feel a dealer or finance company dinged you on the interest rate charged. Refinancing can also be advantageous if you've been paying on your current auto loan for a year or two, and you don't plan to extend your repayment term.

Finally, refinancing is worth pursuing if you had past credit problems that have since been resolved. Your improved credit standing makes you a better bank risk, and should get you a reduced interest rate.

Day 25 Pick a "Pay Down Your Debt" priority strategy.

Many debt counselors and financial advisors tell you to pay off your highest-interest rate credit cards first. But a better strategy is to pay down your debt by *attacking the credit area that bothers you most*. This way you'll stay motivated, and will stick to your payment plan.

Here's the plan:

Decide whether you are most upset by having a big balance, a high interest rate, or multiple accounts.

For example, some people hate high balances. They might not be bothered by an 18% interest rate, but if their card was close to its $10,000 limit, that would cause them anxiety.

Others fret over high interest rates, even if the card has less than a $200 balance.

Still more individuals don't like feeling overwhelmed by too many cards and monthly statements.

Solution: review the list of creditors you created on **Day 3**.

Strategy A: If you want to knock out large debts, attack the card with the *biggest dollar balance first*, regardless of the interest rate.

Strategy B: If you despise high interest rates, start by paying off the card with *the largest rate*, no matter the balance.

Strategy C: If you're tired of juggling too many cards, first pay off the card with *the lowest dollar balance*.

The goal is to attack your area of pain

Pay off the first card as stated above. Then repeat this process to eliminate the debt on each additional credit card.

Let's see how this strategy works in practice. Say you have five credit cards with the following rates and balances:

- American Express – 15.9% interest rate; $2,300 due
- Visa – 9.9% interest rate: $4,800 due
- MasterCard – 13.9% interest rate; $1,400 due
- Macy's – 21.9% interest rate; $750 due
- Discover – 6.9% interest rate; $6,600 due

Scenario 1: I'm going to assume that you're in the first category of consumers: you absolutely abhor seeing big balances, so you'll get really motivated about knocking out your debt with the largest dollar amount due. In this case, you want to attack *the biggest dollar balances* first (Strategy A). That means you'd first pay off that Discover Card: It has the biggest balance: $6,600. Note that you're paying off Discover first, even though it actually has the lowest interest rate attached to it. After Discover, you pay off the Visa bill ($4,800), then American Express ($2,300); MasterCard ($1,400); and finally Macy's ($750).

Scenario 2: Let's say it drives you nuts to see that you're being charged tons of interest on your purchases. This time, your goal is to pay off *the highest-interest rate* debt first (Strategy B). So your prioritized repayment schedule looks like this: Pay off Macy's first. It's got that hefty 21.9% interest rate. Then pay American Express. It's carrying a 15.9% interest rate. MasterCard would be your next target; it's got a 13.9% interest rate. The Visa bill follows, with a 9.9% interest rate. And the last credit card you'd pay would be Discover, which has a relatively small 6.9% interest rate.

Scenario 3: Are you feeling overwhelmed and stressed out simply because you have too many accounts and you're finding it hard to juggle all of them? If this describes you, then your best bet is to start knocking out the number of credit cards with balances. You do this by paying off the cards with *the smallest dollar balance* first (Strategy C). Put into practice, here's how your repayment plan would go: The Macy's bill gets paid first, because that's the smallest total bill outstanding at just $750. Then you pay off the MasterCard ($1,400 due), your American Express card ($2,300 due), that Visa bill ($4,800), and lastly your Discover card, on which you owe $6,600.

What This Technique Does & Does Not Accomplish

You probably noticed that in two of the cases – Scenario 2 and 3 – my "Pay Down Your Debt" priority strategy resulted in consumers paying off the highest-interest rate debt (that 21.9% Macy's card) first. But in Scenario 1, the debtor isn't told to attack the highest interest rate debt. In fact, in the first example, the Macy's bill is the last one to get paid. What's the reason for this?

Unconventional Wisdom

The reason is that this strategy isn't based on conventional wisdom.

Almost all financial planners and many credit counselors tell their clients to pay off the highest interest rate debt first. I don't recommend that as a blanket strategy for every consumer. In the examples I provided, it just so happened that two of the scenarios resulted in the highest rate debt being retired quickly. But the reality is that simply telling someone to pay off their high rate debt first is like recommending that a person with multiple symptoms of the flu take some nasal decongestant to relieve their runny nose. Sure it might cure part of their problem, but if the person is really complaining about having aches and pains, or chills then hot flashes, giving him or her a quick fix for a runny nose is still going to leave the individual wanting for a better solution that they can live and function with.

The same is true for people sick with debt. They can't all possibly employ the same exact approach and do equally well. Everyone is different. And I'm betting that people deep in debt also don't want a band-aid to a problem that's really not bothering them. What they want is for the pain to go away: plain and simple. So they need to attack the area that hurts them or bothers them – financially, psychically, whatever – and then keep pressing on to relieve that area of discomfort.

At the end of the day, that is what will keep a person motivated to continue with their debt repayment plans. Think about it this way. Let's say you're in a rush to get somewhere. You're on a sales call and you don't want to be late for this important appointment. But as you're hurrying along from the parking lot into an office building, you feel something bothering you in your shoe. Good grief! You're thinking: I can't be late; I've got to make a crucial presentation. So what do you do? Do you stop to take whatever is in your shoe out, or do you keep moving?

Let's envision for a minute that you keep going. Ultimately, you get there on time and you make your presentation. But you're not quite as sharp as you wanted to be because, frankly, that darned woodchip or whatever it was in your shoe kept bothering you the whole time.

Rewind this mental picture, and this time, let's say you do, in fact, stop for just enough time to dislodge the item in your shoe. Ahhhhh! You think, "Now that's more like it." You hustle on indoors and go on to make a great presentation, unhampered by any physical pain or discomfort. At the end of the day, I think most people are like the person in this second situation. Given a choice, they'd rather relieve their pain *right now* and get on with the rest of their lives.

Will my "Pay Down Your Debt" priority strategy mean every consumer will always pay as little as possible in interest? No, it doesn't ensure that at all. It does, however, give every indebted person the chance to limit – in their own way – the emotional cost of debt, by empowering them to reclaim their refinances, in a method that's most appropriate and comfortable for them.

Day 26 Weigh the pros and cons of entering a debt management program.

If you get nowhere negotiating with your creditors, you're drowning in debt, you've analyzed your budget, cut back on expenses, have implemented the suggestions found in *Zero Debt*, and have *still* concluded there's no way you can afford to pay all your obligations, the good news is that a debt management program may help. The bad news is that many of them might also hurt you.

Credit Counselors: Friend or Foe?

Every year, about nine million consumers seek help from debt counseling agencies. The typical person in a debt-management program earns about $30,000 a year, is college educated and has credit card debts of about $16,000. Obviously these individuals are in a bind. Unfortunately, the very places they go for help – credit counseling agencies – sometimes make their situations worse. From 1999 to 2003, complaints about the credit counseling industry skyrocketed by 590%, according to the Better Business Bureau. The IRS is now auditing 50 credit-counseling agencies to see if they deserve their tax-exempt status. The Federal Trade Commission and five state attorneys general are suing AmeriDebt. Two other companies, Amerix and Cambridge Credit Counseling, are being looked at by a Senate subcommittee. All have denied wrongdoing. Still, Congress is examining many debt management companies for a variety of alleged wrongful practices including:

- taking clients money and then not paying their bills
- charging unreasonably high startup/monthly fees
- not disclosing to consumers what fees are going to the debt management company vs. towards bills

Shop around and you'll find that some debt consolidation companies make outrageous claims, even going so far as to promise they'll "fix" your credit report virtually overnight. "Any quick-fix company is probably too good to be true," says Fair Isaac spokesman Ryan Sjoblad.

The main problem with the $7 billion debt management industry is that, over the past decade, it has undergone a drastic transformation that is not in consumers' best interests. Let me tell you about the roots of this industry and explain how it now operates. Then I'll tell you the Do's and Don'ts of using a debt management program, in case you decide you need this service.

Traditional Credit Counseling On the Decline

There was a time when people with overwhelming money problems would go to a credit counselor and receive quality advice, help and personal finance education. A person struggling to pay his or her bills might've been signed up for a free class on budgeting, taught the value of saving money for a rainy day, or counseled about how credit cards work. Unfortunately, all that has changed. Lots of programs that used to be free now impose charges. And if you seek help today for your debt woes, nine times out of 10 you won't get traditional "credit counseling," which was educational in nature. Instead, you're more likely to be funneled into a "debt management program", where your bills are consolidated and you're put on a repayment plan. The problem is that lots of people may not need to enter a debt management plan, also known as a DMP. What many consumers really need is financial education; they need to learn how to manage their budget, credit and spending.

The reason the vast majority of debtors are guided into debt management programs is that these plans are a source of revenue for credit counseling agencies. Despite the fact that most of them are non-profits, they still need money to operate. And they get some of that money from consumers who are on monthly repayment plans.

The Financial Ties That Bind

Unbeknownst to most consumers, credit counseling agencies also get most of their operating expenses from credit card companies in the form of payments known as "fair share" contributions. Believe it or not, it was the credit card industry that actually set up the whole credit counseling industry a few decades ago. The goal was to make sure people with large debts didn't go bankrupt – thereby writing off all their bills and never paying their creditors a dime. Instead of that happening, credit card companies realized it was better to let people arrange settlements, where they could have reduced payments, pay lower interest rates, and get late fees eliminated. So creditors funded credit-counseling agencies – helping themselves and helping consumers avoid bankruptcy. The payments credit issuers make to debt counseling agencies actually come from you. Whenever you make a payment under your debt management program, your creditor takes a certain percentage of that money and uses it to pay your credit-counseling firm. Credit issuers used to give debt management companies "fair share" payments of about 15% of a consumer's debt. Now most creditors make contributions of just 6% to 9% of a person's debt.

The Coalition for Responsible Credit Practices is a new organization comprised of credit counseling agencies, business leaders and others who want to reform the credit counseling industry. Michael Barnhart, the Coalition's executive director, asks: "How can consumers be confident that they are receiving accurate, unbiased advice from agencies that are beholden to creditors for a significant portion of their revenue?" His conclusion: "They obviously cannot."

How Debt Management Programs Work

With most debt management programs here's what you'll have to do: cut up your credit cards; agree to not open any new credit accounts, and make regular payments to the credit counseling agency. They negotiate with your creditors to get your bills slashed and consolidate your debts, allowing you write one monthly check to the agency, which, in turn, sends the money to each of your creditors. Most debt management plans last three or four years.

Do's and Don'ts of Debt Management Plans

I recommend that you first try to negotiate with your creditors on your own. If that fails, and you can't meet your bills despite your best efforts, you may be a good candidate for debt consolidation – as long as you first educate yourself about the process and the debt management or credit counseling company you hire to work on your behalf.

Don't think that just because a company is a non-profit it is "better" than for-profit groups. For starters, most debt counseling agencies are non-profit, but many have ties to for-profit entities. Also, non-profit status tells you nothing about an agency's quality of service. Don't sign any contracts until you get detailed feedback about what your repayment plan will look like and what your fees will be. Don't enroll in any program that costs more than $50 to set up or has monthly fees higher than $25. Don't go with a company that only seems to be pushing debt management plans, or that doesn't seem interested in fully hearing your situation. Some suggest DMPs inside of 15 minutes. Better companies talk to you for at least 30 minutes or an hour to get a complete picture of your finances. Also, don't give your bank account information to a debt-counseling firm before you've signed a contract. And finally, don't respond instantly to aggressive marketing pitches – like Spam in your email inbox, Internet advertising or late-night television ads. Instead, do your homework *before* contacting a credit counseling company. By the way, Fair Isaac officials say that entering a DMP does not hurt your credit score, despite what you may have heard.

Do check out a potential debt management firm by contacting the Better Business Bureau. Do call your state Attorney General's office to see if there are any complaints or ongoing investigations against the company. Do ask about the company's standing with the local Chamber of Commerce. If you feel comfortable with what you learn, then go ahead and contact the company. Do avoid agencies with large fees; some are has high as 10% of your monthly payment. Do ask about all your alternatives. Do inquire about the agency's full range of services. Do insist that everything be spelled out in black and white. And if you ever feel cheated, do report any abuse to the Federal Trade Commission.

Some of the better-known debt-counseling organizations are the National Foundation for Credit Counseling, parent company of Consumer Credit Counseling Services (CCCS) of America, and MyVesta. CCCS is the oldest credit counseling service in the U.S. MyVesta is a former credit-counseling agency that now provides only educational services. Their addresses, telephone numbers, and Internet web sites are listed at the end of this book in Appendix A.

The credit counseling industry continues to grow by leaps and bounds. Just do a Google search on the phrase "credit counseling" and you'll get more than 1.1 million hits. Ditto for the term "debt management." And because Congress may pass a federal law requiring anyone who files bankruptcy to first receive debt counseling, the industry is poised for even more explosive growth.

I also encourage you to read a landmark study – the first of its kind – published about the credit counseling business in April 2003. The report is called "Credit Counseling In Crisis: The Impact on Consumers of Funding Cuts, Higher Fees and Aggressive New Market Entrants." It was done by the Consumer Federation of America (www.consumerfed.org or 202-387-6121) and the National Consumer Law Center (www.nclc.org or 617-542-8010). You can download the report free of charge from either group's web site. Or you can request a copy be mailed to you for $30 (paid in advance by check only). It details the pros and cons of credit counseling.

Day 27 Evaluate your existing insurance coverage.

Make sure you have adequate protection for your home and auto, as well as life and disability insurance. This step will strengthen your finances and protect you and your family. The American Council on Life Insurance suggests life insurance coverage of five to seven times your annual salary. Visit www.quickquote.com or call 800-867-2404 to shop for rates. Remember that good credit can translate into lower insurance premiums as well.

And don't think that life insurance is only for people who work full-time either.

Sophia Lezin Jones was once surfing the Internet when a pop-up advertisement solicited her to buy life insurance. Not one to normally respond to such offers, Lezin Jones nevertheless did answer the ad – and now she's glad she did.

A mother of two small boys, Lezin Jones' youngest son, Luke, was born on Thanksgiving Day. She later hopped onto a web site and purchased a $500,000 life insurance policy to protect her family in the event of her death.

"I just felt a big sense of relief," Lezin Jones says. "Now, at least if something happens to me, (my husband) Rich can hire somebody," to take care of the numerous responsibilities she handles daily.

You see, Lezin Jones is a stay at home mom. While she doesn't generate cash income for her family, the value of the services she provides day in and day out are enormous. Those chores include feeding and dressing the children, shuttling her three-year-old son, Jude, to pre-school each day and administering medicine to the kids when necessary.

"All of these things would still have to be done," if she were to die, Lezin-Jones says, in explaining why she opted for life insurance.

In a lot of ways, Lezin-Jones, who lives in West Orange, NJ, is the exception to the rule. Experts estimate that only a tiny fraction of the nation's stay at home parents buy life insurance – even though it could prove just as valuable to their families as to the families of working parents. Moreover, most Americans – in or out of the workforce – are believed to be significantly under-insured.

While the average U.S. household has an income of $49,628, the typical American household has life insurance of only about $196,000, industry statistics show.

So how much protection do you need if you're not bringing home cash income? Statistics – and thus, the advice in this regard – vary wildly. Jeremy White, a CPA in Paducah, KY, did some research to figure out the value of the services provided by a stay at home. His conclusion: the typical at-home mom renders about $60,000 in annual services.

Meanwhile, financial planner Ric Edelman, who runs Edelman Financial Services in Fairfax, VA, believes an at-home mother's services are worth far more. According to Edelman, the 17 occupational duties a mother carries out – everything from childrearing to managing household finances to resolving family emotional problems – are more adequately valued at $508,700 in wages. (Edelman arrived at that figure by adding up the median annual salaries of the 17 occupations).

Experts do generally agree, however, that for most stay-at-home moms and dads, term life insurance is your best option. Compared with permanent life insurance, term life insurance is the most affordable and often most appropriate. It protects you for a specific time frame, such as a 10- or 20-year period, and the premiums are fixed.

If you're a stay-at-home parent, you should know that some companies cap the amount of insurance they sell to you at $250,000. In Lezin-Jones' case, she was able to purchase twice that amount for around $400 a year. She got the increased protection after explaining to her insurer that she plans to re-enter the workforce in the next few years.

To learn more about life insurance, and to comparison shop for the best prices, check out any of the following web sites:

www.accuquote.com
www.quotesmith.com
www.insweb.com
www.insurance.com

Financial advisors at www.insure.com also offer a comprehensive way to evaluate your specific life insurance needs. The guidelines they suggest are based on a variety of factors, including your short-term needs (for things like outstanding debts and emergency expenses); your long-term needs (for expenses such as mortgage payments); education (to cover your dependents' college tuition); your family's maintenance needs (to pay for child care, food, clothing, utility bills, insurance and transportation) and your current assets (including existing savings, stocks, bonds, mutual funds and other life insurance).

Five Types Of Insurance That You Don't Need

Although I advocate buying insurance as a way to protect your family's interest, I also think there are some forms of insurance that are largely unnecessary. They are:

1. Hospital indemnity Insurance
It can cost a few hundred dollars per year, however, it only provides you roughly $100 per day of cash coverage to pay for expenses if you're hospitalized. That's not a lot when you consider that the average hospital stay costs about $1,200 a day.

2. Extended warranty/extended contract insurance
This policy is offered anytime you buy electronics or big-ticket items like DVD players or refrigerators. Usually the cost is very high and not worth it. Plus, when you buy on credit, the credit card company often extends the manufacturer's warranty.

3. "Specific-health" insurance policies
This insurance protects you in the event you get cancer, suffer a stroke, or develop some specific disease. The problem is that this type of insurance is too narrow in terms of the coverage it provides, and these policies often have many exclusions.

4. Life insurance for children

Life insurance is meant to replace the income of the person who dies, to take care of that person's heirs. Unless your kid makes a ton of money, or is in some way earning the family's primary income, life insurance for children is a total waste of money.

5. Flight insurance

It only pays off if you die or get badly injured in a plane crash. And statistically the chances of that happening are extremely small. Don't confuse this coverage, though, with trip interruption or travel cancellation insurance, which might come in handy once in a while.

Day 28 Draw up a will.

Wills aren't just for rich people. A last will and testament is a must for anyone with minor children. You also need a will if you have anything at all of value – even sentimental value, like your wedding ring, a favorite coat or a treasured book collection. In the event of your death, a will tells the state (and your family) who should take care of your minor children, and who should get what, in terms of your assets. Wills can also help reduce family squabbling and the drama of grieving relatives arguing over how to divide your things. If you don't have the money to pay an attorney to create a will, for now use software programs or buy the ready-made wills found in office supply stores such as Staples, OfficeMax and Office Depot. For online forms or step-by-step software to make a will, go to:

www.nolo.com (800-728-3555)

www.ezlegal.com (800-822-4566)

www.legalzoom.com (323-962-8600)

www.uslegalwills.com (866-317-9306)

Don't procrastinate! Draw up a will at once. Save money if you must by creating the will yourself with a store-bought form. But I still recommend having an attorney give it a final look to make sure it conforms to your state law. Also, remember to have two witnesses sign your will and get it notarized by a notary public who can put a seal on the will. To get motivated about making your will, think about your loved ones and fill out the form on the next page. You can also get this at www.themoneycoach.net. Go to the downloads section of the "Free Info" area, and then click on the proper PDF.

Get the Will to Draw Up A Will

I need an updated will because I would like to give my _____

(insert item)

to _____in the event of my death.

   (insert friend or relative's name)

I would also like to leave my_____ to _____.

                     (insert item)   (insert name)

I need a will because I have a minor child (or children) named

_____.

(insert name(s) here)

And to be a responsible parent, I want to appoint a guardian to ensure his/her (or their) well being in my absence.

I need a will because upon my death, I wouldn't want to burden

_____, my _____

  (insert name)   (insert relationship, i.e. *sister*, *husband*, etc.)

with decisions that I should have made while I was alive.

Week Number 5

This week you will:

- Open a "hands-off" account and set up an automatic savings plan
- Prepare yourself to become a positive financial role model
- Address any other special circumstances in your life concerning money or credit

Day 29 Open a "hands off" account and set up an automatic savings plan.

Go open a savings account at a credit union without a lot of branches, a bank that's far away from your home and job, or a small financial institution that doesn't offer ATM cards. Your goal is to have a "hands off" account where it's somewhat difficult or inconvenient to access your money. This way, you won't constantly withdraw it. Also, have your employer set up automatic payroll deductions from your paycheck to go into that "hands off" account. Even if it's just a small amount, start your automatic savings plan immediately. If you don't get your hands on the money, you won't miss it as much! The earlier you start saving and investing the better. If you save/invest $150 a month, earning 10% here's how it will grow:

	Actual $ Saved	Your $ w/interest at each year-end
Year 1	$1,800	$1,980
Year 2	$3,600	$3,967
Year 3	$5,400	$6,267
Year 4	$7,200	$8,808
Year 5	$9,000	$11,615
Year 10	$18,000	$30,726
Year 20	$36,000	$113,905
Year 30	**$54,000**	**$339,073**

See the power of compounded interest?

Day 30 Prepare yourself to become a positive financial role model.

If you're like most adults, you probably want your children, or any youngsters around you, to develop good financial habits. But if you're like the typical American, you may also struggle when it comes to being a good financial role model for our youth. A study by Northwestern Mutual revealed that 71% of parents feel that children should begin learning about money no later than the 1st grade. Yet, five in 10 parents say they do not set a good example when it comes to handling money, and that they are not capable of properly teaching their children to manage money. To boost your financial literacy, enroll in an adult education class on personal finances. To educate yourself about investing, join the National Association of Online Investors (www.naoi.org), which has great online study courses. For resources, fun games, tips and ideas for teaching youngsters about money, log onto www.nefe.org or call the National Endowment for Financial Education at 303-741-6333.

The Northwestern Mutual survey found that less than 40% of parents talked about credit cards, loans and debt, and their own family finances with their kids. Fewer than one in four parents (23%) talked to their children about how to invest.

When asked why each topic was not raised for family discussion, most responded, "Children have no business knowing this." Others said they "didn't think of it" or that they considered their children too young to broach these issues.

But researchers also suggest another theory.

"It is almost certainly lack of confidence with their own financial management skills that keeps parents from discussing some of the more complex, and key, money issues with their children," says Mark Schug, professor and Director of the University of Wisconsin-Milwaukee Center for Economic Education.

If you are a parent or educator who would like more information and free materials on personal finance education, check out www.themint.org. That web site, jointly run by Northwestern Mutual and the National Council on Economic Education (www.ncee.net), offers practical tips, lesson plans, newsletters and interactive challenges to help teach kids of all ages about money.

Most experts caution that you can't rely on the school system to teach your kids about money and finance.

"The lack of financial literacy in this country is really a shame," says Bob Barry, former chairman of the Financial Planning Association. "Unfortunately, most schools are doing a terrible job of teaching the youth the basics about finance and investing."

Financial professionals nationwide echo Barry's sentiments.

For example, experts at the Greenwood Village, Colorado-based National Endowment for Financial Education sometimes find it difficult to get school districts throughout the country to allow NEFE representatives to come into their schools and provide proper financial training and education. NEFE (www.NEFE.org) has a cadre of capable and energetic volunteers on hand, and it offers financial education free of charge. Still, the organization frequently hears from administrators "we already teach that." A review of the existing curricula, though, most often reveals a shell of a program or very basic things, like how to open a bank account.

By contrast, NEFE teaches Americans – mainly high school students – practical money management skills, such as setting financial goals, developing a budget and understanding the pros and cons of using credit. The organization also introduces teens to more sophisticated subjects, including insurance, investments, taxes, and retirement planning. While NEFE offers a fine program, financial literacy isn't just for the youth. Most adults sailed through high school and even college without knowing a stock from a bond. As a result, many of us could also benefit from getting a solid financial education.

If that describes you, consider turning to the Securities Industry Association, Wall Street's trade group. The SIA has teamed up with the Stock Market Game Program ™ to introduce the *SIA Investor Challenge*. The Stock Market Game targets the youth. But the *Challenge* is a hybrid educational initiative geared toward the adult crowd. "Investors consistently want more knowledge, education and tools to help them learn about investing. And we're giving them one," says SIA spokesperson Margaret Draper.

The SIA Investor Challenge can be found at www.SIAInvestor.com. The game is interactive and gives you access to experts who walk you through the basics, like asset allocation, evaluating risk, and portfolio diversification.

Best of all, you get a hypothetical $100,000 and the right to "trade" any security listed on the NYSE or Nasdaq, so you practice investing before putting your own funds at risk. At the end of the *Challenge*, you total your gains (or losses). Hopefully, by the time you do actually trade with "real" money, any investing blunders you make will be few and far between. Also, with any luck at all, your kids will emulate your successes – and avoid your mistakes.

There are a few other companies and initiatives that I consider enormously helpful for any parent, educator or adult that wants to teach kids about money – or even improve their own financial knowledge. One of them is a fabulous web site, www.moneysavvygeneration.com, where you can get a special four-chambered piggy bank for kids. Youngsters can put coins in each of the four slots, which are labeled "save," "spend," "donate," and "invest." I have these educational piggy banks for both of my kids.

Citigroup has one of the most comprehensive financial education programs I've encountered. For adults, there's Citi Cards' "Use Credit Wisely" program, as well as its "Hablando de Credito" or "Let's Talk About Credit" education effort for Spanish-speaking consumers. Both offer a wealth of personal finance tools, help and information. In 2004, Citigroup launched a 10-year, $200 million campaign to support financial literacy programs around the globe. Additionally, its Smith Barney unit has a great Young Investors Network that's good for middle school and high school students. The youngsters in the Network are taught fiscal responsibility, they learn how to calculate their college expenses, and they participate in a stock-portfolio contest, among other activities. To learn about the full range of personal finance initiatives sponsored or run by Citigroup, visit the company's web site at www.citigroup.com. Then click on the "Financial Education" button found in the "Corporate Citizenship" section.

Day 31 Address any other money woes, credit issues, or special financial circumstances.

Throughout *Zero Debt*, I've attempted to cover a host of common situations that consumers with credit or money management issues face. But there are also a host of other economic dilemmas, and you may still need to address some of these special situations to achieve financial freedom. Read on to find out if any of these scenarios apply to you. Or if the information you learn in the following pages could help someone you know, be sure to share it with him or her.

Bankruptcy: Your Last-Ditch Option

The number of debt-laden consumers seeking bankruptcy protection from their creditors has reached unprecedented levels. In 2003, 1.6 million households declared bankruptcy.

If you're one of the many consumers filing for bankruptcy – or considering it – please think long and hard before you take this extremely drastic step. My experience in talking to consumers has been that most attorneys specializing in this area are quick to advise people to file for bankruptcy. On the other side, many credit counselors may tell you to never, ever file for bankruptcy. Obviously, there's no one-size-fits all solution here. But I believe that even if you're drowning in debt, bankruptcy should be a last resort – contemplated only after you've truly exhausted all other possibilities. You should also know a few basic facts before you entertain the prospect of a bankruptcy. For starters, filing for bankruptcy isn't free – or even cheap. Expect to pay $500 to $1,000 or more in court filing fees and attorneys costs, depending on where you live and the complexity of your situation. Bankruptcy also doesn't get rid of all types of debt. For instance, spousal and child support obligations are not dischargeable in bankruptcy; and in most cases, neither are student loans and tax debts.

In *Everyone's Money Book on Credit*, author and personal finance expert Jordan Goodman notes that declaring bankruptcy is no panacea, because a bankruptcy filing remains on your credit for seven to 10 years and hampers your ability to secure future credit.

"Potential employers and landlords may also learn that you declared bankruptcy," Goodman says. "Therefore, bankruptcy is not exactly the fresh start that many lawyers advertise."

Another consideration: bankruptcy may really haunt you much longer than the decade that it is listed on your credit report. How so? Some job or credit applications ask you: Have you *ever* filed for bankruptcy? Even if your bankruptcy was 15 years ago, you're legally required to say "Yes." If you lie, you've just committed a crime.

Delinquent Taxes: What To Do About Them

If you owe back taxes to the government, a little-known measure of recourse to you is to propose an "Offer in Compromise" to settle your delinquent tax bill. Most taxing authorities will accept a lump sum or a payment plan for less than the amount you owe to settle old taxes. Some of the entities that will consider an "Offer in Compromise" are the Internal Revenue Service, the Franchise Tax Board, and the State Board of Equalization. They'll even be willing to negotiate to lower any late fees and interest charges that have accumulated, along with self-employment or Medicare taxes that may be due.

If you've lost your job, retired, got sick, had a business that went bust, or have filed bankruptcy, you have pretty good odds of getting a tax authority to accept your "Offer in Compromise" – or at least be amenable to working out some mutually acceptable deal with you. The reason is that the Offer in Compromise program was designed to collect back taxes that the government might otherwise never collect. In some cases, people who owe tax debts have been able to pay anywhere from 10 cents to 50 cents on the dollar when they work out an "Offer in Compromise" as a settlement.

If you'd like to learn more about this topic, read up on the subject at www.nolo.com.

Helping Aging Parents With Their Finances

If you have elderly parents, it should come as no surprise that the older Mom and Dad get, the more vulnerable they are to a host of medical and financial challenges.

CPAs recommend that you discuss medical and financial issues with your aging parents periodically. Changes in their health or financial situation, as well as ever-changing tax laws, could affect how they plan for and protect their future.

Unfortunately, too many of us shy away from talking to our parents about money matters – even when an older parent's deteriorating health starts to greatly impact his or her financial well-being.

If you've ever found it difficult to talk to your parents about their finances, follow these tips to open the lines of communication, and to safeguard your parents' financial health.

- Acknowledge Your Parents' Perspective – And Your Own

Susan Richards, a certified financial planner in Chicago and the author of "Protect Your Parents and Their Financial Health … Talk With Them Before It's Too Late" believes it's natural to feel squeamish inquiring about how well (or how poorly) a parent is doing financially. The reason? Having that conversation "changes the dynamic of the parent-child relationship" she says. That feels like a role reversal, in which you are now the caretaker, and that's likely to be unfamiliar and uncomfortable territory.

Additionally, you may feel ill equipped to manage your own finances, let alone give your parents guidance about how to manage theirs. If this is the case, seek professional help from a qualified financial advisor.

- Realize that helping your parents is a process, not an event

Ask your parents what small steps you can take to continually aid them. Maybe you can pay their bills online, see that their bank accounts are properly credited for deposits, or do their weekly shopping. Engage them in the process, though, by inquiring directly about exactly where they need assistance in handling their day-to-day finances.

Tip: If your parents receive a Social Security check each month, you should visit a nearby Social Security Administration office and ask to be made a representative payee. The SSA will conduct an investigation and, if you check out, the agency will appoint you to act on your parents' behalf. You can then use those funds to set up automatic monthly payments for your parents' recurring bills.

- Know Where Important Records Are Located

Ask your parents to prepare a list of their assets, liabilities and other pertinent financial information. As gently as possible, make it clear that you need to know where relevant documents are – such as a will, medical cards or insurance policies – in the event something happens to them.

- Consider drawing up appropriate legal documents

But don't just give your parents a piece of paper (or even worse, mounds of paperwork) to fill out. That will just overwhelm them. Instead, have a conversation about what they would like to do with their assets, how they would like their affairs to be handled in the event of their incapacitation, and what they would prefer to happen upon their death.

The California Society of Certified Public Accountants recommends that adult parents weigh a number of options, including establishing durable powers of attorney, trusts, living wills and joint bank accounts. All these documents require your parents' signature while they are still capable of conveying those powers to you or someone else. Many legal experts favor a durable power of attorney. That allows a parent to give another person, usually a spouse or a child, permission to handle their financial affairs if the individual in question suffers an illness such as a stroke or develops a condition like Alzheimer's. An ordinary power of attorney is not valid once a person becomes incapacitated.

- Take advantage of appropriate resources and government agencies

Contact the Social Security Administration for a report on your parents' earnings history along with estimates of their retirement, disability and death benefits, if they don't have it already. Call 1-800-772-1213 or visit the web site www.ssa.gov. The form you'll need is called a Request for Earnings and Benefit Estimate Statement.

Finally, The Eldercare Locator, (800) 677-1116, is a nationwide, directory assistance service that helps you find an array of services of the elderly – everything from home care to transportation to legal and social services. The Eldercare Locator is a public service of the Administration on Aging, (www.aoa.dhhs.gov) and the U.S. Department of Health and Human Services.

Payday Loans: 'Credit' You Must Never Accept

I usually try to refrain from giving absolutes when dispensing personal finance wisdom. But this is an area where I want to be extremely clear: Never, ever, ever get a payday loan.

If you've taken a payday loan before, then you probably know that you're being charged loan-shark rates – worse than most loan sharks charge as a matter of fact. But for those of you new to this world, here are the facts.

- Payday loans are short terms loans made by financial "institutions." These loans are designed to "tide people over" until they get their paycheck.

- Payday loans work like this: A customer needs money before he gets his paycheck next Friday. To make ends meet he goes to a payday lender who verifies that the individual has a legitimate job and a bank checking account. The customer gets a $300 "loan" – immediate cash in exchange for writing a postdated $300 check to the payday lender. This check is cashed once the individual's payday rolls around. But the payday lender doesn't actually give the consumer $300. Instead the customer will get $255; the other $45 is the fee or interest cost associated with taking this payday loan.

- On an annualized basis, payday loans like that work out to be about 400% per year. Some have effective Annual Percentage Rates (APRs) of nearly 800%.

- The average person who gets a payday loan gets one per month, or 12 per year.

- Regulators and consumer protection groups are all worried about how payday lenders operate, especially their aggressive collection practices. The Federal Trade Commission, Consumers Union and the Consumer Federation of America have all expressed concern about the payday loan industry.

- Cash-strapped consumers often "rollover" their payday loans multiple times, and wind up paying more than

1,000% in interest, according to a study by Georgetown University researchers.

- By partnering with certain financial institutions, and skirting various statutes, payday lenders are able to get around state usury laws that prevent lending entities from charging sky-high interest rates.

Bottom line: If you think regular old debt collectors bound by federal laws are hard to deal with, you definitely don't want to fool around with payday lenders and subject yourself to their shenanigans. Even if you're desperate for money to pay your debts, seek any other source of cash you can, such as a pay advance from your employer or a loan from a family member, rather than resort to payday loans.

If you've taken all the advice in *Zero Debt*, I know the last month has been fruitful and eye opening. Keep track of your progress. And do let me know about your victories in conquering your debt and mastering your finances. To share your story or to ask me a money management or personal finance question, email me at lynnette@themoneycoach.net. Please also visit my web site, www.themoneycoach.net, to learn more smart ways to save, spend, or invest your money.

Here's wishing you Zero Debt status and financial freedom for a lifetime!

Appendix A: Credit Bureaus

Equifax
P.O. Box 740241
Atlanta, GA 30374
www.equifax.com
800-685-1111

Trans Union
P.O. Box 2000
Chester, PA 19022
www.transunion.com
800-916-8800

Experian
P.O. Box 2002
Allen, TX 75013
www.experian.com
888-397-3742

Innovis
PO Box 219297
Houston, TX 77218-9297
www.innovis-cbc.com
800 540 2505

Debt Counseling Firms

National Foundation for Credit Counseling
(Parent organization of CCCS)
8605 Cameron Street, Suite M2
Silver Spring, MD 29207
www.nfcc.org
800-388-2227

Myvesta
P.O. Box 7153
Gaithersburg, MD 20898-7153
www.myvesta.org
800-MYVESTA

Appendix B: Sample Settlement Letter

Your Name
Your Address
Your City, State and Zip Code

Date

Name of Customer Service Rep
ABC Credit Card Company
ABC Credit Card Company Address
Their City, State and Zip Code

Via Certified Mail, Return Receipt Requested #_____

Re: Account# 444-333-222 with your company

Dear _____:

Per our telephone conversation of today, this letter is to confirm that I will send $250 to ABC Credit Card Co. as "Payment in Full" to settle the balance due on the above-referenced account.

Within seven days of receiving my $250 payment, ABC Credit Card Co. will delete from my credit report any negative references related to this account, and will update its records with the credit bureaus to reflect that my account has been "Paid in Full" or "Paid as Agreed."

Your signature below will verify your acceptance of these terms. After you return to me a signed copy of this agreement, I will immediately forward my $250 payment.

Thank you for your assistance with this matter.

Sincerely,   Date Agreement Signed: _____

_____   _____
Your Name   ABC Credit Representative

Appendix C: Sample Cease & Desist Letter

Your Name
Your Address
Your City, State and Zip Code

Date

Collection Agent Name
XYZ Collection Agency
XYZ Collection Agency Address
Their City, State and Zip Code

Via Certified Mail, Return Receipt Requested #_____

Re: Account# 123-456-789 with ABC Creditor

Dear _____:

As I have told you in numerous telephone conversations, I am unable to pay the above referenced debt due to my job layoff.

I hereby assert my right, under Section 805-C of the Fair Debt Collection Practices Act, to request that you cease any further communication with me.

Sincerely,

Your Name

Appendix D: The 30-Day Zero Debt Challenge!

How many items can you do in 30 days?

Write down your start date, a Y for Yes, N for No, and the date you finish each task

Start Date:	Done?
Day -- Action Item	Yes/No
1. Call 888-5-OPT-OUT	
2. Vow to 'stop digging'	
3. Put all debts in writing	
4. Order credit report	
5. Negotiate with creditors	
6. Switch credit cards	
7. Exceed min. payment	
8. Dispute credit errors	
9. Learn legal rights	
10. Stop harassment	
11. Thwart ID theft	
12. Set up filing system	
13. Face the truth	
14. Create SMART goals	
15. Analyze cash sources	
16. Scrutinize spending	
17. Set realistic budget	
18. Cut spending 10 ways	
19. Adopt 5 life changes	

20. Adjust W-4 withholdings	
21. Sell unwanted stuff	
22. Generate more income	
23. Get home equity line	
24. Refinance auto loan	
25. Pick debt payoff plan	
26. Consider debt mgmt.	
27. Evaluate insurance	
28. Draw up a will	
29. Open 'hands off' acct.	
30. Become a role model	

CONGRATULATIONS!

I want to hear all about your progress! E-mail me at lynnette@themoneycoach.net to tell me what steps you've completed. After you finish "The 30-day Zero Debt Challenge," no matter how many items you've finished, I want to send you a Certificate of Achievement. ☺

If you want to get an 8 ½ by 11-inch copy of "The 30-Day Zero Debt Challenge," please visit the "Free Info" section at www.themoneycoach.net and follow the link to the proper PDF. Print out this free download, then put it up on your wall to remind yourself of the action steps that will get you on the road to financial freedom *in just 30 days*!

Appendix E: Consumer Resources

Web Sites

www.bankrate.com

www.cardweb.com

www.capitaloneautofinance.com

www.citigroup.com

www.consumer.gov/idtheft

www.countrywide.com

www.lowermybills.com

www.moneysavvygeneration.com

www.myfico.com

www.practicalmoneyskills.com

www.salliemae.com

www.thedollarstretcher.com

www.themint.org

www.themoneycoach.net

Books

Credit After Bankruptcy by Stephen Snyder (2002)

Everyone's Money Book on Credit by Jordan Goodman (2002)

The Complete Idiot's Guide to Beating Debt by Steven Strauss and Azriela Jaffe (2003)

The Motley Fool Personal Finance Workbook by David Gardner and Tom Gardner (2003)

The Ultimate Credit Handbook by Gerri Detweiler (2003)

Your Money or Your Life by Joe Dominguez and Vicki Robin (1999)

Index

<u>NOTES</u>